TESTIMONIALS

TO WHOM IT MAY CONCERN

RE: Dr. Rao Konduru's Publications:
   Reversing Obesity
   Reversing Sleep Apnea
   Reversing Insomnia

   Dr. Rao Konduru, PhD is a patient of mine who has suffered from chronic diabetes for most of his life. He also suffered from uncontrollable obesity, sleep apnea and chronic insomnia for the past 3 to 4 years. He has managed to reverse all of these conditions by taking non-pharmacological and science-based natural measures with great success. He has created 3 how-to user guides/books with regard to how he achieved this, and I recommend these books for anyone suffering from these conditions.

Sincerely,
Dr. Ali Ghahary, MD
Brentwood Medical Clinic
Burnaby, British Columbia, Canada

At first we read "Reversing Obesity" another book by Dr. RK, and we found it better than the best books in the weight-loss industry. His recipe for the pre-workout meal "Egg White Omelet" is a major highlight. Anyone can lose weight by eating whole foods and by following the simple instructions for rapid weight loss method illustrated by Dr. RK.

After that we read his second book "Reversing Sleep Apnea" and we were blown away by its extremely impressive contents. Dr. RK convinces you beyond a shadow of a doubt that obstructive sleep apnea can be reversed simply and easily by losing weight. He has covered all the important therapies that a sleep apnea patient would ever need.

Then we read his third book "Reversing Insomnia" and his writing keeps getting more and more interesting. Dr. RK describes exactly where the planet Earth is located in our universe, and how it creates the daytime and nighttime by rotating on its own axis and by revolving around the sun. He divides the 24-hour master biological clock into two parts, one for the daytime and the other for the nighttime, and instructs the insomniacs what to do exactly as the day progresses and as the night progresses. By simply following his instructions, naturally, and without ever using sleeping pills, anyone can reset his/her master biological clock, and sleep like a baby within a few days. What a wonderful book!
 - Prime Publishing Co.
New Westminster, British Columbia, Canada

This book "Reversing Insomnia" is the simplest, and perhaps the safest way to cure chronic insomnia. Dr. RK has done all the spadework and leaves the rest of us to reap the benefits. All one has to do is read and follow the simple do-it-yourself instructions.

Hats off to Dr. RK and his impressive research. He figured how the master biological clock embedded in the brain works, and came up with an effortless and natural method to permanently cure chronic insomnia. He applied and tested his discovery on himself. It took him just 3 days to reverse his chronic insomnia after suffering from it for over 3 years.

After reading the entire book, I wholeheartedly believe it is the best cure for the sleep disorder. One, because it hardly takes time to cure the insomnia; two, because it has no side effects; and three, because sleeping pills are a complete waste of money.

It really works. So, just give it a try!

- Ms. Muriel D'Souza, Advertising Copywriter, Vancouver, British Columbia, Canada

---

++

REVIEWS

Please do not ignore reviews. Please read all reviews thoroughly.
You can learn a lot by reading through the reviews below:

++

Jade
5.0 out of 5 stars The Natural and Effortless Insomnia Treatment That Works!
Reviewed in the United States on February 5, 2021
Verified Purchase

Until the electricity was discovered and distributed for modern living, and before the houses, workplaces and streets were illuminated by electricity, our ancestors used to work hard under the Sunlight during the day, and used to sleep in pitch-black dark houses during the night. Our ancestors did not suffer from chronic insomnia like we do now by living under bright and powerful electric lamps in houses, workplaces and on streets. This is the major cause of current-day chronic insomnia.

This book "Reversing Insomnia" teaches that by living under the Sunlight or bright lights during the day (for 12 hours), and by living strictly in the pitch-black darkroom during the night without ever exposing to bright lights (for another 12 hours) at least for a few days, it is possible to reset the Master Biological Clock, and to reverse chronic insomnia. This is the fundamental principle based on which the method of reversing chronic insomnia has been derived and outlined in this book.

All we need do is reset "the Master Biological Clock" by doing some simple exercises nicely outlined in this book in a simple language in order to reverse chronic insomnia.
If you read, understand and follow carefully all 24 instructions outlined in the Main Article of this book in Chapter 1, you can reverse chronic insomnia in 3 days to 3 weeks, depending on how seriously and sincerely you implement this method without breaking the rules.

I reversed it in 3 days. It is the one 100% natural method. All those prescription sleeping pills and OTC sleep aids are a mere waste of money, unnecessary and they further ruin your health. Believe it or not, this natural method works but you must try it seriously and sincerely by exercising self-discipline at least for a few days! All sleep clinics should adopt this natural method. All insomniacs must be free from insomnia by using this book.

++

Wang Inhee
5.0 out of 5 stars Nice!
Reviewed in the United States on November 8, 2019   Format: Kindle Edition
I would highly recommend everyone to read this book. This book gave me a lot of information. This book is awesome to read and I think this book is the best book of this topic, and I really appreciate this book.

++

++

Jailyn *5.0 out of 5 stars* Helpful Steps to Treat Insomnia!
Reviewed in the United States on November 4, 2020 Verified Purchase

Computers, laptops, iPads, iPhones, tablets, cell phones, many other gadgets, and bright light bulbs at home, workplace, and outdoors, they all attack our eyes with "artificial bright light late at night," tricking our body's master biological clock into living at a perpetual high noon (12 o'clock in the daytime), mimicking the sunlight. The brain therefore enters into a state of confusion, and becomes unable to recognize that it is the night time, and does not secrete the natural melatonin as usually from the pineal gland (which is a fluid-filled space located on the back of the brain), thereby developing insomnia or chronic insomnia. Natural production of melatonin from the pineal gland of your brain is essential to fall asleep and to maintain deep sleep at night, especially late at night.

"Reversing Insomnia: The Instant Guide to Sleeping Like A Baby Tonight" provides us very simple "Do-It-Yourself Instructions" on how to reset the master biological clock and how to reverse chronic insomnia through simple exercises so that the melatonin production from pineal gland becomes normalized. Just follow the 24 simple instructions outlined in this course in the first chapter, and you will be able to reset master biological clock, and reverse chronic insomnia. It is possible to reverse it in 3 days if you try it seriously. Right from the first night, when you start living alone in a pitch-black room, you will start yawning excessively with an instant feeling of sleeping. That means you are on your way to reversing chronic insomnia.

Reversing Insomnia book has taught me so many wonderful things and deeds to naturally treat and reverse my chronic insomnia, and so I adore this book!

++

rohit joshi *5.0 out of 5 stars* Real Insomnia Cure Is At Your Fingertips!
Reviewed in India on March 4, 2020 Verified Purchase

I have been living with insomnia for a long time, and those sleeping pills are not at all helping me. My body created resistance to sleeping pills, and they stopped working. I may have to increase the dosage of sleeping pills in order to make them work, but it would be dangerous to do so, as this book suggests.

This effortless sleep method and natural self-treatment explained nicely in the book "Reversing Insomnia" is very easy to practice, and it works like a miracle right from the first day. All I needed was Chapter 1 to reverse my insomnia. I read Chapter 1, I did not even read the whole book, and I started seeing results immediately.

The weather where I live is very hot, and I can easily expose to sunshine during the day as explained in this book, which has helped boost my sleep at night. I have maintained darkness at my home easily by turning off all the lights. I just used my torch light to move within my small house. Voila, everything worked like a miracle as explained in this book when I started living in pitch-black room. I started yawning and was tempted to go to bed early. I slept on my side as this book suggests, and woke up in the morning fully refreshed.

I am so grateful for all those 24 instructions detailed in Chapter 1, and very useful information outlined in the other chapters. Every chapter has interesting information. All that information about caffeine control in Chapter 7 will also be very useful to me. I genuinely recommend this book to whoever suffers from chronic insomnia. This natural method works, just try it out!

++

+++

Jack mckeever
5.0 out of 5 stars   Middle-of-the-Night Insomnia Cure Is In This Book!
Reviewed in the United Kingdom on March 12, 2020
Verified Purchase

We often worry about lying awake in the middle of the night - but it could be good for you, some sleep specialists and researchers say. A growing body of evidence from both science and history suggests that the eight-hour continuous sleep may be unnatural.

Dr. THOMAS WEHR'S RESEARCH ON SEGMENTED SLEEP: In the early 1990s, a psychiatrist Dr. Thomas Wehr conducted an experiment in which a group of people were plunged into darkness for 14 hours every day for a month. It took some time for their sleep to regulate but by the fourth week the subjects had settled into a very distinct sleeping pattern. They slept first for four hours, then woke for one or two hours before falling into a second four-hour sleep. Though sleep scientists were impressed by the study, among the general public the idea that we must sleep for eight consecutive hours still persists.

This book suggests that "Segmented Sleep" should not be practiced intentionally. But if your sleep is divided into several segments during the night, stay peacefully in a relaxed mood as if everything was normal without panicking. Chapter 4 is dedicated for this kind of very interesting research-based topic. Living alone in the DARK ROOM (PITCH-BLACK ROOM) during the nighttime, without any kind of light (a battery-powered lamp can be used during walking only), would significantly help improve your sleep and combat chronic insomnia. The spontaneous melatonin production by the pineal gland located in your brain is the key to attaining a good night's sleep (Do not take artificial melatonin pills).

If you are suffering from middle-of-the night insomnia, please read the INSTRUCTION # 24 of Chapter 1 "How to treat Middle-of-the-Night Insomnia," and follow the treatment method explained there step-by-step. You will be successful if you follow those guidelines carefully.

+++

Chandan
5.0 out of 5 stars   Yes, it is possible to reverse chronic insomnia in 3 days!
Reviewed in India on January 26, 2021
Verified Purchase

Yes, it is possible to reverse chronic insomnia in 3 days. I did it and I am sure anybody can do it. The instructions given in this book are very simple to follow, and any layperson can understand.

The complete book "Reversing Insomnia" gives all scientific details on how master biological clock works, and how it regulates the production of melatonin from the pineal gland located in the brain. You need to reset your master biological clock if you want to cure your insomnia exactly as explained in this mini book. I have read both books "Reversing Insomnia" and "Reversing Insomnia in 3 Days."

I recommend all insomniacs to please read the complete book "Reversing Insomnia' by the same author. You will be amazed to cure yourself the chronic insomnia in 3 days without using any sleeping pills. The method is completely natural, and it works for anybody.

+++

isha
5.0 out of 5 stars This Natural Method Is Easy to Implement!
Reviewed in India on January 26, 2021
Verified Purchase

The natural method illustrated in this book to cure chronic insomnia is easy to implement, easy to follow, and easy to get positive results. I understood all 24 instructions presented in Chapter 1, and practiced "Reversing Insomnia" procedure, and I was able to completely reverse my chronic insomnia in less than 3 days, and started sleeping like a baby thereafter.

THIS NATURAL METHOD IS EXPLAINED IN ONE PAGE: As a matter of fact, you don't even have to read all 24 instructions. Chronic insomnia treatment is summarized in one page. Please refer to Page 6 of this mini book titled "Reversing Insomnia in 3 Days: The Instant Guide to Sleeping Like A Baby Tonight." Or just click on the green link "Insomnia Treatment Summarized in One Page" in the Active Table of Contents of the Kindle eBook. By reading and by following the simple instructions (very simple exercises) provided in one page only, you can easily reverse chronic insomnia in 3 days. Try it out. You will be successful, happy, and will start sleeping like a baby thereafter.

+++

Poonam
5.0 out of 5 stars You Can Reverse Chronic Insomnia In 3 Days, Assured!
Reviewed in India on January 28, 2021
Verified Purchase

You can reverse chronic insomnia in 3 days as I reversed it. The process of reversing insomnia begins right on the first night when you turn off all ceiling lights, and when you start living in the pitch-black darkness after 7 pm.

By living under the sunlight or bright lights during the day, and by living strictly in the dark during the night without exposing to bright lights, it is possible to reverse chronic insomnia. This is the fundamental principle based on which the method of reversing chronic insomnia has been derived and outlined in this book.

+++

Anna Zoe
4.0 out of 5 stars Appreciating content
Reviewed in the United States on November 6, 2019   Format: Kindle Edition
I was recommended this book by a sleep specialist. It is helping me a lot. I can't thank the authors enough for the wonderful work they did writing it. They created a clear path to help with sleep issues; easy to follow directions, a bit of tough love and wonderful suggestions that make sense. Each step is explained well.

+++

++

Bilal Khalil
5.0 out of 5 stars Amazingly Simplified Insomnia Cure!
Reviewed in the United Arab Emirates (UAE)   www.Amazon.ae
November 6, 2020

I have wasted a lot of time and money by visiting sleep clinics, sleep specialists, and by buying sleeping pills, OTC products and sleep remedies, and nothing helped me as good as this amazing and simple treatment outlined in this book.

I just read page 10 in which chronic insomnia treatment procedure is summarized briefly in one page so that a layperson could easily understand, and follow those instructions rigorously, and results were outstanding. This treatment worked for me, as I am now free from insomnia.

As the book suggests, it is important that you should follow these simple instructions strictly if you want this treatment work for you right away. I did exactly want the procedure instructed me to do in page 10. I also read all 24 instructions of Chapter1. The procedure is very simple and natural. When I followed all instructions of this procedure step-by-step, my Master Biological Clock was reset within a few days, and the melatonin production became normal and usual and switched me to natural sleep mode within a few days.

I now know what to do exactly as the day begins, as the day progresses & as the day ends, as the night begins, as the night progresses & as the night ends. It is very easy to be accustomed to this natural self-treatment. I will live like that for the rest of my life, and I will be sleeping like a body every single night. Thanks to this amazing "Reversing Insomnia" book and to the author!

++

Reema
5.0 out of 5 stars Sleep Apnea Patients also Suffer from Insomnia!
Reviewed in India on March 19, 2021
Verified Purchase

I also suffered from chronic insomnia when I suffered from sleep apnea. Sleep apnea causes insomnia although insomnia does not cause sleep apnea. Whenever the blood oxygen level (so called SPO2) falls too low due to large apneas, the brain wakes the sleep apnea patient up so that the patient can breathe in oxygen (otherwise the patient could die in sleep). If the brain wakes up too frequently, a sleep apnea patient simultaneously suffers from insomnia. Many people with severe sleep apnea also suffer from chronic insomnia.

There is no such doctor who could understand and treat both sleep apnea and insomnia at the same time. My sleep clinic doctor never addressed my insomnia problem, and all those insomnia specialists whom I visited in the past don't seem to understand what sleep apnea is, except writing a prescription for sleeping pills. Dr. RK's books (Reversing Sleep Apnea and Reversing Insomnia) teach how to reverse both sleep apnea and insomnia at the same time. I found both books are extremely useful.

++

++

Deanna Maio
5.0 out of 5 stars Awesome Insomnia Course That Is Fully Natural!
Reviewed in the United States on August 30, 2020
Verified Purchase

This insomnia course made perfect sense to me as I was able to reverse my chronic insomnia in a few days by reading through chapter 1.

Common sense tells us that we must perfectly be awake during the day, and perfectly be asleep during the night. That was the reason why our planet Earth by rotating on its own axis every day (24 hours) and by revolving around the Sun in 365 days (1 year) creates day and night (12 hours for the day and 12 hours for the night).

During the day we are supposed to be perfectly awake and work hard under the sunlight, and during the night we are supposed to rest and sleep under the moonlight in the dark. The Master Biological Clock located in our brains is designed in such a way that it works perfectly well when we live under the Sun or bright lights during the day, and rest and sleep during the night by staying in the dark.

But the modern technology created electricity and everything changed. People started abusing the technological advancements by spending a lot of time sitting under artificial bright light. This kind of activity tricks your body's biological clock into living a perpetual noon, mimicking the bright sunlight. Therefore the pineal gland located in your brain fails to secrete natural melatonin. As a result, a person develops circadian rhythm disorder. This is the reason why some people fall asleep during the day and stay awake in the night, and feel the symptoms of underlying sleep disorder called "Chronic Insomnia".

++

Steve_M
5.0 out of 5 stars A Must-Read Book for All Insomniacs!
Reviewed in the United States on June 15, 2021
Verified Purchase

It is the safest way to cure chronic insomnia from its root causes. The author of this book has done an impressive research and, all the spadework, and leaves the rest of us to reap the benefits. All you need do is read and follow the simple do-it-yourself instructions.

This book explains how the master biological clock embedded in the brain works, and the author came up with an effortless and natural method to permanently cure chronic insomnia. He applied and tested his discovery on himself. It took him just 3 days to reverse his chronic insomnia after suffering from it for over 3 years.

After reading the entire book, I practiced it on myself, and it works exactly as it says.
I wholeheartedly believe that it is the best cure for the chronic insomnia developed due to sleep disorder. You don't need to go to a sleep specialist who would prescribe you an anxiety pill. This natural method has no side effects, and remember the sleeping pills and anxiety pills are completely waste of money and worthless. You must read this book if you suffer from chronic insomnia.

++

++

Wellness Books
5.0 out of 5 stars Effortless Sleep Method & Natural Insomnia Cure!
Reviewed in Canada on March 4, 2020
Verified Purchase

I recommend this "REVERSING INSOMNIA" book to all people suffering from sleeplessness or chronic insomnia.

Dr. RK'S BOOKS ARE ALL MUST-READ HEALTH BOOKS: I have read his intriguing book "Drinking Water Guide". His book "Permanent Diabetes Control" is wonderful. All his health books are extremely impressive, extremely interesting, extremely useful, and directly applicable to current-day health problems that many people face today. I recommend that both medical doctors and naturopathic doctors should read these books, and benefit from the contents. All his books are science-based and practical guides. His extensive scientific research experience is clearly visible in these books.

He teaches everything so nicely step-by-step by dividing the book's contents into many headings, sub-headings and paragraphs so that a layperson can easily understand his teachings. He always convinces the reader with logic by making simple calculations that make sense. All his teachings are science-based with simple mathematics and attractive tables, showing the innovative experiments he conducted at the comfort of his home on his own body, resolving his own complex health issues with natural methods, without ever using traditional prescription drugs being prescribed by doctors. This book is no different.

I have read and enjoyed his three well-written and well-organized books "Reversing Obesity, Reversing Sleep Apnea, and Reversing Insomnia." These books are extremely useful to medical community. All contents are directly applicable to my own health problems I have been facing for years, and extremely useful. I am now using his books and am sure these books will help me controlling my weight gain, my mild sleep apnea and help cure my insomnia (sleeplessness) as well. I offer my hearty congratulations to the author Dr. RK.

++

Antonie Brown
5.0 out of 5 stars Recommended
Reviewed in the United States on November 6, 2019
Format: Kindle Edition
I purchased this book for my female friend who has trouble getting a full nights sleep. She often wakes up in the middle of the night and stays awake for hours. She read a lot of books on the subject. And she thought that this book provided the best information. The book is easy to read.

++

++

Daniele D'Alessio
5.0 out of 5 stars This Course Will Reset Your Master Biological Clock!
Reviewed in the United Kingdom on August 30, 2020
Verified Purchase
This is an amazing natural method that works for any insomniac. If you are suffering from chronic insomnia or sleeplessness, you most probably have developed the circadian rhythm disorder, which means your master biological clock, also known as the suprachiasmatic nucleus (SCN), located in your brain was disturbed and shifted from normal mode to the disturbed mode. As a result, your brain is unable to recognize and distinguish the difference between the daytime and the nighttime, and therefore the secretion of melatonin from your pineal gland has become stagnant or unregulated. In order to get out of this dilemma, you need to reset your master biological clock by practicing the very simple and easy-to-follow exercises (24 instructions) described in this book.

By living under the sunlight or bright lights during the day, and by living strictly in the dark (in a pitch-black room) during the night without ever exposing to bright lights, it is indeed possible to reverse chronic insomnia. Our ancestors used live like that until and before the electricity was discovered.

This mini course is designed to teach you everything step-by-step on how to do it correctly at the comfort of your home. If you read, understand and practice sincerely and seriously all instructions detailed in this mini course, you could be a winner, and abolish your chronic insomnia in 3 days. This mini course will reset your master biological clock, if you practice it seriously, and you will be sleeping like a baby thereafter. There is absolutely no need to visit sleep specialists and more importantly sleeping pills are unnecessary.

++

Akash
5.0 out of 5 stars Amazing Insomnia Treatment!
Reviewed in India on February 9, 2021
Verified Purchase
This is an amazing book that contains amazing insomnia treatment. At the end of Chapter 1, this book warns that a person may not reverse chronic insomnia if he/she suffer from (i) elevated cortisol level and/or (ii) overactive thyroid function. IT IS TRUE IN MY CASE.

When I tried this method for the first time, it did not work. I later found out that I had elevated cortisol level (beyond the normal range). I took a natural supplement to treat my elevated cortisol level, and started monitoring my AM cortisol and PM cortisol regularly once every 3 months (with my doctor's requisition). After 6 months to one year of natural treatment, my cortisol level dropped down to normal level.

Then I started using this natural method to reverse my chronic insomnia (Living under the Sunlight or bright lights during the daytime, and living in the pitch-black darkness during the nighttime). Right from the first night, after I tried to practice this method, I began yawning between 9 pm and 10 pm as the method worked perfectly, and put me to sleep naturally when I maintained pitch-black darkness in my bedroom.

++

Reversing Insomnia In 3 Days

The Instant Guide To Sleeping Like A Baby Tonight

THIS EFFORTLESS SLEEP METHOD AND NATURAL SELF-TREATMENT IS THE ANSWER

To Cure Chronic Insomnia By Offsetting the Root Causes Without Ever Using Any Sleeping Pills!

LEARN WHAT TO DO EXACTLY

DURING THE DAY	DURING THE NIGHT
• As the Day Begins	• As the Night Begins
• As the Day Progresses	• As the Night Progresses
• As the Day Ends	• As the Night Ends

EASY-TO-FOLLOW & DO-IT-YOURSELF INSTRUCTIONS
To Cure Chronic Insomnia Overnight!

This Guide Will Make You A Self-Taught Insomnia Guru!

Author: Rao Konduru, PhD

IMPORTANT NOTE

CHRONIC INSOMNIA TREATMENT IS SUMMARIZED IN ONE PAGE,
PLEASE REFER TO PAGE 6 IN THE PAPERBACK.

BY FOLLOWING THESE SIMPLE INSTRUCTIONS PROVIDED
IN ONE PAGE ONLY (You don't have to read the whole book),
YOU CAN EASILY REVERSE CHRONIC INSOMNIA IN 3 DAYS.
IT IS ABSOLUTELY POSSIBLE!

However please read and understand
the 24 detailed instructions of the full course.

FOREWORD

The Master Biological Clock located in the brain of every human being coordinates all the body clocks so that they are in synch. Each body clock has its own function. The Master Biological clock is made up of a group of about 20,000 nerve cells in the brain called Suprachiasmatic Nucleus (SCN), and is located in the hypothalamus, just above the optic nerve, and its major function is to control circadian rhythms.

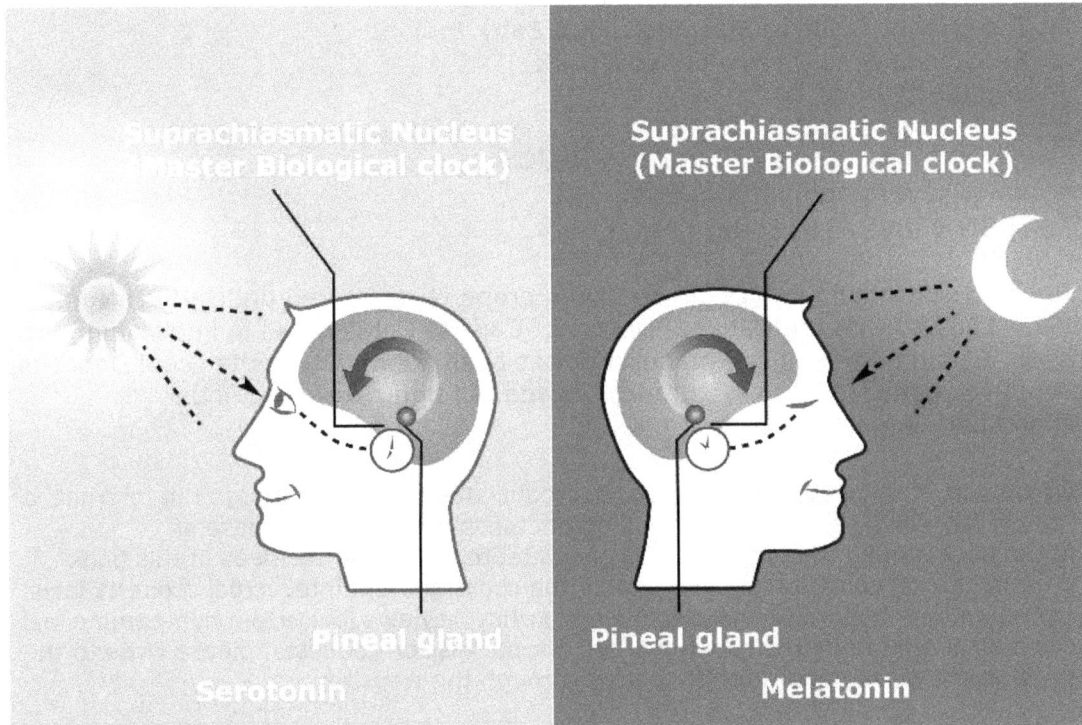

Figure 1 Sunshine promotes serotonin and moonlight promotes melatonin.

Sunlight, by passing through the retinas of our eyes, enters the hypothalamus and tells the Master Biological Clock the time of the day. The intensity of the sunlight is highly responsible for the production of serotonin that induces the feeling of joy. Moonlight and the intensity of darkness signal the Master Biological Clock, and in turn the pineal gland, that it is nighttime and it is the time to secrete melatonin. The melatonin production tells your body that it is time to sleep. Melatonin does not induce sleep, but it is up to the individual to understand the body's language (it is time to sleep), and to stay in a quiet and calm darkroom, to relax by suppressing all thoughts of the mind, and to go to bed in an attempt to sleep.

By living under sunlight or bright lights during the day, and by living strictly in the dark during the night, without exposure to bright lights, it is possible to reverse chronic insomnia. This is the fundamental principle based on which the method of reversing chronic insomnia has been derived and outlined in this book.

It is not that difficult to treat chronic insomnia. You absolutely do not need sleeping pills. If you read, understand and follow carefully all 24 instructions outlined in the Main Article of this book, you can reverse chronic insomnia in 3 days to 1 week (maximum 2 weeks). The reversal of insomnia begins right on the first night. You will feel it, yawning excessively as the night progresses. Believe it or not, Dr. RK reversed his chronic insomnia in 3 days after suffering from it for more than 3 years. The method outlined in this book in the first chapter is extremely effective.

- Prime Publishing Co.

COPYRIGHT

Book Title: Reversing Insomnia in 3 Days
Sub-Title: The Instant Guide to Sleeping Like A Baby Tonight!
Author: Rao Konduru, PhD (Also Called Dr. RK)
Publisher: Prime Publishing Co.
Address: 720 – Sixth Street, Unit: 161
               New Westminster, BC, Canada, V3L-3C5
Website: www.reversinginsomnia.com
ISBN #   ISBN 9780973112092

Dr. Rao Konduru's Publications	
1. Permanent Diabetes Control	www.mydiabetescontrol.com
2. The Secret to Controlling Type 2 Diabetes	www.mydiabetescontrol.com
3. Reversing Obesity	www.reversingsleepapnea.com/ebook2.html
4. Reversing Sleep Apnea	www.reversingsleepapnea.com
5. Reversing Insomnia	www.reversinginsomnia.com
6. Drinking Water Guide	www.drinkingwaterguide.com

The paperbacks (softcover books) and Kindle eBooks are available for purchase on Amazon.com for US residents, and on Amazon.ca for Canadian residents.

Reversing Insomnia In 3 Days
It Is Chapter 1 of the Complete Book "Reversing Insomnia"
Please visit www.ReversingInsomnia.com

TABLE OF CONTENTS

Figure 2 An insomniac is sitting on his bed awake in the middle-of-the-night.

Soon, you will be amazed to learn "how to sleep like a baby" by following the effortless and at the same time natural sleep method, self-discovered by Dr. RK who reversed his chronic insomnia in less than a week after suffering from it for more than 3 years!

IMPORTANT NOTE

CHRONIC INSOMNIA TREATMENT IS SUMMARIZED IN ONE PAGE,
PLEASE REFER TO PAGE 6 IN THE PAPERBACK.

BY FOLLOWING THESE SIMPLE INSTRUCTIONS PROVIDED
IN ONE PAGE ONLY (You don't have to read the whole book),
YOU CAN EASILY REVERSE CHRONIC INSOMNIA IN 3 DAYS.
IT IS ABSOLUTELY POSSIBLE!

However please read and understand
the 24 detailed instructions of the full course.

CHAPTER 1: MAIN ARTICLE
INSOMNIA TREATMENT

INTRODUCTION

If you are suffering from chronic insomnia or sleeplessness, you most probably have developed the circadian rhythm disorder, which means your biological clock was disturbed and shifted from normal mode to the disturbed mode.

You have been staying up late in the night, watching too much TV, using desktop computers, laptops, tablets, iPads, iPhones, cell phones and/or other gadgets, spending a lot of time sitting under artificial bright light generated by fluorescent bulbs and LED lights, and reading on electronic screens exposing your eyes extensively to artificial blue light. This kind of activity tricks your body's biological clock into living a perpetual noon, mimicking the bright sunlight. Your body's natural rhythms would therefore be confused and your brain is unable to distinguish between daytime and nighttime. Therefore the pineal gland located in your brain fails to secrete natural melatonin that is needed to tell your body that it is time to sleep. As a result, you develop circadian rhythm disorder. This is the reason why some people fall asleep during the day and stay awake in the night, and feel the symptom of underlying sleep disorder called "insomnia."

If that happens, you need to reprogram your brain in order to reset the biological clock to its normal mode by making some simple lifestyle changes and maintaining the sleep hygiene outlined in this course. By taking appropriate action with willpower and self-discipline, it is possible and in fact very easy to reverse the circadian rhythm disorder in less than a week. Once your circadian rhythm disorder is reversed and your biological clock is adjusted and reset to normal mode, the hypothalamus in your brain signals your body to start producing melatonin, as is usual during the nighttime so that you would be able to sleep like a baby again.

In Order to Treat Your Circadian Rhythm Disorder, You Divide Your 24-Hour Biological Clock into Two Parts: "Daytime and Nighttime." And you should train your brain by informing it what exactly are the daytime hours, and what exactly are the nighttime hours. If you do so, your brain would understand your sleep-wake cycle, correct the circadian rhythm disorder, restore it from the confused state, and act accordingly to re-establish your sleep patterns through producing appropriate melatonin during the nighttime so you would sleep well.

DURING THE DAY	DURING THE NIGHT
◎ DURING THE DAY, YOU ESSENTIALLY LIVE UNDER THE SUNLIGHT WHENEVER YOU ARE OUTDOORS OR UNDER BRIGHT LIGHTS WHENEVER YOU ARE INDOORS.	◎ DURING THE NIGHT, YOU ESSENTIALLY LIVE IN THE DARK BY STAYING AT HOME. ALWAYS STAY INDOORS, AND DO NOT GO OUTSIDE. DO NOT EXPOSE YOURSELF TO BRIGHT LIGHTS.
◎ BY DOING SO, YOU WOULD LET YOUR BRAIN KNOW EXACTLY WHICH HOURS ARE THE DAY. For example 6 am to 6 pm, 7 am to 7 pm or 8 am to 8 pm. Each person is different so you choose your DAY hours.	◎ BY DOING SO, YOU WOULD LET YOUR BRAIN KNOW EXACTLY WHICH HOURS ARE THE NIGHT. For example 6 pm to 6 am , 7 pm to 7 pm or 8 pm to 8 am. Each person is different so you choose your NIGHT hours.

If you live like that, within a few days, your master biological clock will be reset, and you will start sleeping like a baby thereafter. It works like a miracle!

CHRONIC INSOMNIA TREATMENT SUMMARIZED IN ONE PAGE
[By Following the Instructions Provided in This Page Alone, You Can Easily Reverse Insomnia]

You are suffering from chronic insomnia because your body's natural circadian rhythms and therefore your master biological clock disturbed, entered into a confused state, and unable to recognize and distinguish between daytime and nighttime. In that case, you need to reprogram your master biological clock. In other words, you need to train your brain and clearly inform your brain which hours are daytime and which hours are night time by doing the following exercise for a couple of days, or until you reverse your insomnia.

DURING THE DAY
a. During the day, equip your house or apartment with bright lights (no dim lights during the day howsoever), and live under bright lights. Go outside as frequently as possible, and walk on the street, and expose to the Sun while sitting in a beach or park. While walking on the street, look at the sky as frequently as possible desperately searching for the Sun. If the Sun is not visible, look at the sky and clouds. By doing so, you are letting your brain know that it is the daytime.

b. During the day, if it is cold outside, go to a shopping mall as frequently as possible, and walk in the mall. While walking in the mall, look at the ceiling lights as frequently as possible. By doing so, you are letting your brain know that it is the daytime.

DURING THE NIGHT
a. During the night, turn off all bright lights and live in the pitch-dark. Never go out and expose yourself to bright street lights after 7 pm. During the night, always stay home while practicing this Insomnia Treatment and until you reverse your insomnia. Finish your cooking and eating early by 7 pm or 8 pm, and turn off all lights, close all windows and curtains, and don't let the bright light from street lights enter into your house or apartment. By doing so you are letting your brain know that it is the night time.

b. **USE A BATTERY-POWERED LAMP DURING THE NIGHT AFTER 7 pm or 8 pm** while walking within your house or apartment, and turn it off while resting or sitting in the living room, kitchen or bathroom.
c. **You can watch TV by sitting in the dark**, but turn down the volume and turn down the brightness of your TV. By doing so you are letting your brain know that it is the night time.

d. After 9 pm or 10 pm, sleep alone in a pitch-black bedroom. Suppress all your thoughts, relax and sleep. Sleep on your side, not on your back (Side-sleeping opens your airway, improves your breathing and stops snoring). Let there be no noise howsoever, and sleep alone like a baby! **Please do not sleep during the day. If you are sleepy during the day, get out and walk (Go to a shopping mall and walk by looking at ceiling lights).**

BELIEVE ME IT WORKS LIKE A MIRACLE!
If you live like that, within a few days, your master biological clock will be reset, melatonin secretion will be restored, and you will start sleeping like a baby thereafter. You will start yawning excessively right from the first night. It works like a miracle, and you will sleep like a baby! Try it out!

This treatment plan is explained in detail in 24 steps in the following pages. Please read through all 24 steps, understand all concepts, and practice it. You will be successful!

INSOMNIA TREATMENT: PREPARATION
Please Follow These Instructions Strictly & Carefully:
1. LIVE ALONE AT LEAST FOR A WEEK TO TREAT YOUR INSOMNIA:
To try this insomnia treatment outlined below, you must live alone in a quiet place. You should not live with a group, too many family members, children and/or friends who make noise by talking loudly, or by eating and drinking, or by cooking meals and by partying under bright lights during the evenings and late nights.

2. LIVE IN A QUIET PLACE (NO NOISE) TO TREAT INSOMNIA: You should find a quiet room, apartment or house, which is under your own control and where you could live alone without any disturbance caused by other people. There should not be too much noise. Your living place during the night should be extremely quiet and there should not be bright lights during the night. If there is noise coming from neighbors, you should fix that problem by talking to the landlord or you should move to a quieter place. You would essentially be living in an extremely quiet and dark place during the night.

3. YOU COULD LIVE WITH YOUR SPOUSE IF YOUR SPOUSE ALSO UNDERSTANDS AND FOLLOWS ALL INSTRUCTIONS: You could live with your spouse only if the spouse would also follow all the instructions carefully, does not make any noise and would not live under bright lights during the night.

4. PURCHASE AND INSTALL HIGH-WATTAGE CEILING LIGHT BULBS:
Install high-wattage light bulbs (100 Watts) on the ceiling in all rooms (living room, bathroom, kitchen) except the bedroom in your apartment, condo or house wherever you live. These lights should dissipate light as bright as possible so that your eyes could stand and get accustomed to see the things around without any eyestrain. Usually 100 Watts light bulbs should do the job. These lights should have ON-OFF switches so that you could turn off all the lights after 6 pm/7 pm. By doing so you are training yourself to live under bright lights during the day.

5. PURCHASE A BATTERY-POWERED DIMMABLE TABLE LAMP TO BE USED IN THE NIGHT: Purchase a few "Wireless, Battery-Powered, Dimmable & Portable Table Lamps with ON-OFF Switches," and place them one in the bedroom next to your bed, one in the living room, one in the kitchen and one in the bathroom. Many Dollar Stores sell these lamps. Most importantly when you get up and go to the bathroom to urinate during the night, carry the battery-powered lamp with you. Place the lamp away from you on the countertop and do not look at the lamp. Turn off the lamp as soon you get back to your bed or couch. By doing so you are training yourself to live in the dark during the night.

6. TURN DOWN THE BRIGHTNESS OF YOUR TV TO DIM LIGHT:
Using the TV Remote Control, Hit Menu button, scroll down to Brightness. Adjust the brightness by pressing the left arrow and/or right arrow buttons located at the center of the Remote Control. After you have adjusted your TV screen to the desired brightness (close to the lower end of the scale, that is DIM), hit the EXIT button.

7. TURN DOWN THE BRIGHTNESS OF YOUR COMPUTER MONITOR TO DIM LIGHT:
Press the BRIGHTNESS switch located at the bottom of your computer monitor or laptop. The BRIGHTNESS scale appears ranging 0 to 100%. Adjust the brightness to 30% using the up-down arrow buttons on your monitor. After a few seconds, the BRIGHTNESS scale would disappear, and your monitor would operate at DIM light.

8. INSTALL THE F.LUX SOFTWARE (FREE) ON YOUR COMPUTER:

Visit the following website, https://justgetflux.com/, download and install the software program called **f.lux** on your computer (**it is free**). F.lux makes the color of your computer's display adapt to the time of day, warm at night and like sunlight during the day. The program was designed to reduce the eyestrain during the nighttime and to reduce the disruption of sleep patterns.

9a. <u>Quit Alcohol Consumption:</u> If you are a frequent or daily alcohol drinker, you must quit before starting this Insomnia Treatment. Alcohol consumption mostly before bedtime causes insomnia at night and daytime drowsiness or sleepiness. So train yourself to quit alcohol consumption.

9b. <u>Take A Decision Whether To Drink Limited Coffee, Decaf, or Herbal Tea:</u>
Option-I: Consider Quitting Coffee, and Drink Herbal Tea Instead

♦ Overconsumption of coffee throughout the day disrupts your sleep and causes insomnia. For more information about how caffeine disrupts sleep and causes insomnia and chronic pain:

♦ If you believe that caffeine could be causing insomnia, and if you can withstand the coffee withdrawal symptoms, just go ahead and quit coffee. Consider switching to herbal tea. Organic Rooibas Red Tea has no caffeine, gives you energy and tastes good so you can easily adapt to it. Add some organic skim milk or 1% milk to it.

Option-II: Consider Replacing the Coffee with "Decaf Coffee"

♦ Please note that decaf is not 100% free of caffeine. The decaffeination process does not allow to remove more than 97% of the caffeine, meaning that 3% of caffeine is still present in decaf coffee.

♦ So "Decaf Coffee" presents an opportunity for you to consume a tiny or very limited amount of caffeine that could help keep you alert during the day.

Option-III: Consume Optimum Number of Cups of Coffee, Decaf Coffee or Both

♦ A person must research on his/her body and figure out by trial and error how much coffee is too much, and find out the optimum number of cups (1 cup, 2 cups or 3 cups) that could keep him/her alert during the day, and does not interfere with the sleep during the night.

♦ Under any circumstances, do not drink regular coffee or decaf coffee in the afternoon (be very strict). It is known to scientists that coffee could remain in your body up to 12 hours after consumption and could affect your sleep adversely, causing insomnia. So consume all the coffee you need (1 cup, 2 cups, or 3 cups) before noon. Do not consume coffee or any other drinks (Coke, Diet Coke, Pepsi, Diet Pepsi, or other soft drinks) during the afternoon or evening.

♦ During the afternoon, just drink purified water, ginger tea, or organic Rooibas Red Tea. Read CHAPTER 7 to find out the caffeine content of various foods and drinks.

♦ During this insomnia treatment as outlined in this course, even though you find yourself slept well all night long, you may experience afternoon sleepiness. In order to combat the afternoon sleepiness, and to remain alert throughout the afternoon, you should research on yourself and figure out, and consume the optimum amount of caffeine before noon.

♦ **FOR EXAMPLE:** The author of this book (Dr. RK) drinks 1 cup of organic coffee at 7 am when he wakes up in the morning, and then 1 to 2 cups of decaf before 11 am. That would keep him alert during the day, and does not cause afternoon sleepiness or insomnia during the night.

FINAL NOTE OF PREPARATION: By following the aforementioned 9 instructions, you are preparing yourself to live under sunlight or bright lights during the day, and strictly live in the dark during the night. <u>Under any circumstances do not expose yourself to bright lights during the night</u>. This is the fundamental principle based on which the following natural method of "**reversing chronic insomnia**" has been derived.

INSOMNIA TREATMENT BEGINS HERE	
LEARN WHAT TO DO EXACTLY	
DURING THE DAY	**DURING THE NIGHT**
◐ As the Day Begins ◐ As the Day Progresses ◐ As the Day Ends	◐ As the Night Begins ◐ As the Night Progresses ◐ As the Night Ends

DURING THE DAY [7 am to 7 pm]
DURING THE DAY, YOU ESSENTIALLY LIVE UNDER SUNLIGHT WHENEVER YOU ARE OUTDOORS OR UNDER BRIGHT LIGHTS WHENEVER YOU ARE INDOORS.

As The Day Begins
10. Get up early in the morning at 7 am or 8 am whichever is convenient for you. Maintain the same schedule every day to get up in the morning and to go to the bed in the evening.

When You Get Up in the Morning:
a. Turn on all the ceiling lights (let all lights be as bright as possible for your eyes).
b. Turn on the TV (there should be some noise) and turn on your computer/laptop.
c. Walk to the window(s), open all the curtains, and look outside into the light.
d. Look for the rising sun and stare at the sun (if visible) for a few minutes.
e. If possible, get out of your home and look at the rising sun and sky for 5 minutes. If the rising sun is not visible, then look into the sky and clouds for a few minutes.
f. Walk to the kitchen, brew a cup of organic coffee or herbal tea (if you already quit coffee), and add a few tablespoons of 1% organic milk, and drink it.
g. While taking the coffee/herbal tea, walk to your desk, connect to the internet, listen to loud music on YouTube or listen to some music on the radio, check your emails and reply to emails, and turn on your cell phone, read and reply to all text messages, and phone all the important people and talk to them by making noise.
h. After taking the coffee/herbal tea, brush your teeth and take a bath, and wear office clothes and shoes (During the night, you are going to wear pajama and slippers only). If you continue living like that, your brain would recognize that it is daytime whenever you wear office clothes and shoes, and it is nighttime whenever you wear pajama and slippers.

By doing so, you are letting your brain know that the daytime has just started at around 7 am, and you want to remain fully alert and fully awake for the rest of the day till 7 pm.

As The Day Progresses
11. GO OUTSIDE AND EXPOSE YOURSELF TO THE SUN AND/OR BIGHT LIGHTS:
a. Every few hours (20 minutes each time), go out and expose yourself to the sunshine, which would boost your ability to sleep well during the night. Do not over-expose to the sun (that could cause skin cancer). If you do not see the sun, look at the sky and the clouds.
b. Go to a shopping mall, several times during the daytime, and walk there. While walking, look at the bright lights of the ceiling. By doing so you are letting your brain know it is daytime.
c. When you are at home, during the daytime, make sure all the bright lights of the ceiling are on in the living room, kitchen and bathroom. Try to look at the ceiling lights every now and then.
d. Never go into the bedroom, during the daytime, and never lie on the bed in the bedroom. Never take any naps by going into the bedroom or by lying in the bed. Bedroom is always a dark room that you would use only during the nighttime (between 7 pm and 7 am).
e. If you feel like napping or feel drowsy, quickly get out of your house or apartment and walk on the street. While walking on the street, look at the sun once every few minutes. If you do not see the sun, look at the sky and the clouds. By doing so you are letting your brain know that it is daytime, and you do not want to sleep.

EXPOSURE TO SUNLIGHT DURING THE DAY BOOSTS YOUR SLEEP AT NIGHT!

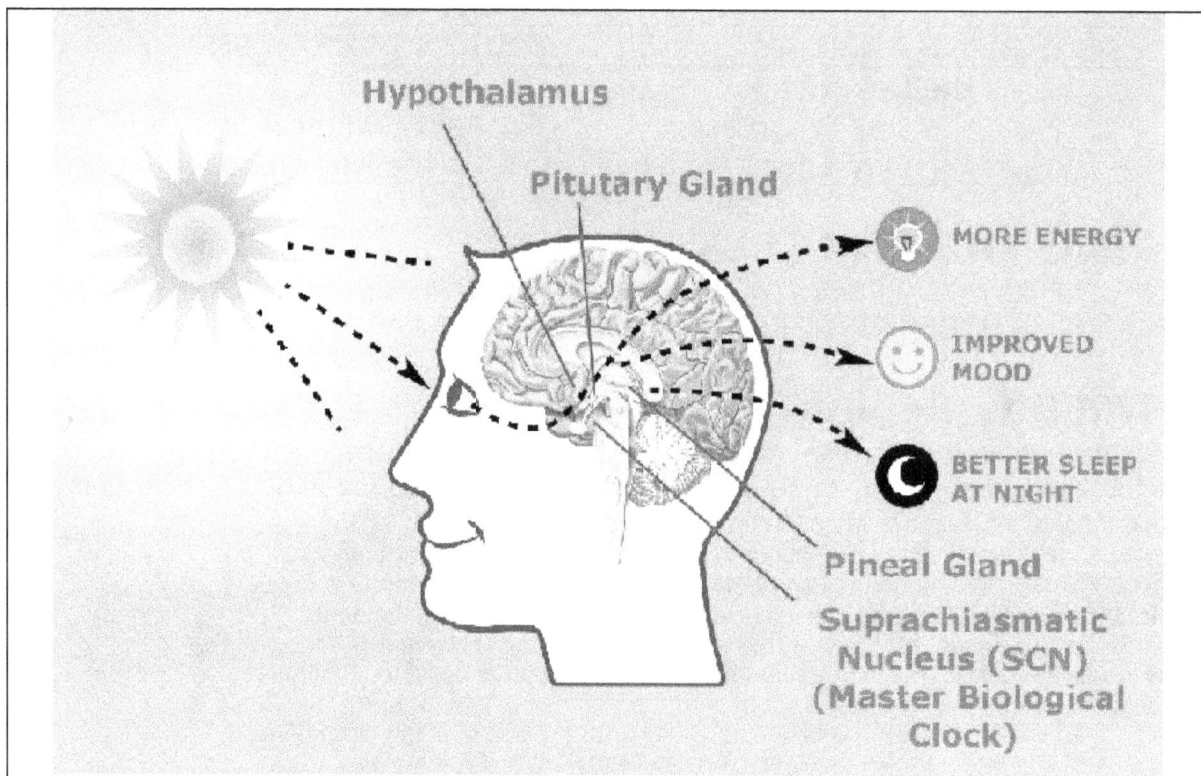

Figure 1.1 Exposure to Sunlight.

a. Sunlight or moonlight is sensed by the retinas of your eyes.

b. The pineal gland secretes melatonin at night upon the orders of the master biological clock, also called suprachiasmatic nucleus (SCN), located in your brain. The melatonin secretion is regulated by a rhythm-generating system located in the suprachiasmatic nucleus (SCN) of the hypothalamus, which in turn is regulated by sunlight or moonlight.

c. Exposure to the bright sunlight every day during the daytime regulates your circadian rhythm, provides you more energy, secretes melatonin appropriately, and boosts your sleep at night.

Figure 1.2 Exposure to the bright sunlight during the daytime boosts your sleep at night.

12. Exercise Every day
♦ Exercise improves muscle stimulation, reduces stress, and improves sleep at night.
♦ Exercise improves quality of sleep, gives freshness and improves self-image.
♦ Exercise in general makes you feel refreshed and helps you live with good mood.
♦ Exercise increases the efficiency of the heart and lungs, and keeps the body alert.
♦ Exercise on a regular basis also lowers total cholesterol & LDL cholesterol levels.
♦ Exercise helps you lose weight, keeps your body weight normal, and also improves your overall health.

You can exercise in the following three possible ways:
(i) You can go out and walk on the road (or street) for 1 hour, and expose to the Sun while sitting in a beach or park. While walking on the street, look at the sky as frequently as possible desperately searching for the Sun. If the Sun is not visible, look at the sky and clouds. By doing so, you are letting your brain know that it is the daytime.

(ii) You can go to a large shopping mall and walk there for 1 hour if the mall permits. While walking, look at the ceiling lights of the shopping mall as frequently as you can. By doing so, you are letting your brain know that it is the daytime.

(iii) You can go to a gym and exercise for 1 hour. You can run on a treadmill, ride a bike, do elliptical or other. After finishing your workout, go out and sit on a bench outside for some time and look at the Sun, sky and clouds. If the Sun is not visible, look at the blue sky and clouds. By doing so, you are letting your brain know that it is the daytime.

Burning calories can be accomplished through a variety of exercises such as walking and running, running on a treadmill, elliptical or biking in the gym, swimming, aerobics, bicycling, bowling, skiing, skating, stretching, playing tennis and other sports of your preference.

While any type of exercise would do the job, "walking, treadmill, swimming and biking" are most suitable and comfortable to most people.

13. Cook Your Own Meals at Home With Organic Whole Foods:
Do not consume processed foods and refined foods in restaurants on a regular basis.

14. Lose Weight if You are Overweight or Obese:
It is a proven fact that when your body resumes normal weight, your health disorders could disappear. If you are suffering from chronic insomnia, you most probably have gained weight. You must work hard to lose weight and make sure that your body weight is normal. You can find out your excess body weight and if you are overweight or obese by calculating the Body Mass Index (BMI) or by monitoring your body fat percentage. You should lose weight until your Body Mass Index or body fat percentage goes down to normal.

$$\textbf{BMI} = \text{Weight (Kg)} / \text{Height (m)}^2$$

For the complete weight-loss course, refer to another Book "REVERSING OBESITY (Self-Discovered Weight-Loss Method Illustrated)" by Dr. RK who not only reversed his insomnia in a week (in 3 days actually) but also reversed his obstructive sleep apnea by losing weight. Please visit www.reversingsleepapnea.com/ebook2.html for "Reversing Obesity," and www.reversingsleepapnea.com for "Reversing Sleep Apnea."

Given below are some weight-loss recommendations:

WEIGHT LOSS RECOMMENDATIONS (by Dr. RK)

Create a 2000-Calorie Diet (low fat, high protein) with organic whole foods only.

   a. Learn how to recognize whole foods, processed foods and refined foods.
      Eliminate processed foods & refined foods from your diet. Eat only whole foods.
      Stop eating out in restaurants. Start eating home-cooked meals made from whole foods.
   b. Learn how to count calories (if it is difficult for you, use measuring cups).
   c. Learn how to read labels when you shop for groceries. Eliminate foods with
      preservatives, artificial colors & flavors, saturated fat, trans fat, MSG, etc.
   d. Drink 8 to 16 cups of purified water every day.
      Do you know? Extreme weight loss contestants drink 16 cups of water per day.
   e. Take apple cider vinegar (2 to 3 tbsp) in a cup of water using a straw before meals.
      It acts as a hunger suppressant, improves digestion and promotes weight loss.
   f. Eat organic Kamut Puffs as a snack whenever you feel hungry in between means.
   g. Eat an omelet made with organic egg whites and veggies as a pre-workout meal.
   h. Exercise every day for an hour after eating the pre-workout meal.
   i. Minimize salt and oil consumption in all your meals.
   j. Sleep for at least 8 hours per night (If you have sleep apnea, sleep with the CPAP).
   k. Record your weight and waist size every day when you wake up in the morning.

Go on with the 2000-Calorie Diet along with daily exercise for 2 to 3 months.
If you do not lose significant amount of weight, then lower the daily calorie intake by 500 calories and continue for another 2 or 3 months.

   a. After 3 months, create a new diet by reducing 2000 calories to 1500 calories.
   b. After 3 more months, create a new diet by reducing 1500 calories to 1000 calories.
   c. After 3 more months, create a new diet by reducing 1000 calories to 500 calories.
      Do not try a diet below 500 calories.

For the complete weight-loss course, refer to another Book titled REVERSING OBESITY (Self-Discovered Weight-Loss Diet Illustrated) by Dr. RK who reversed his obstructive sleep apnea by losing weight. http://www.reversingsleepapnea.com/ebook2.html.

MY WEIGHT-LOSS JOURNAL: When I reduced my daily calorie intake from 2000 calories to 1000 calories, and stopped eating all junk foods (processed foods and refined foods), maintained high willpower and high self-discipline, my body fat (mostly belly fat) melted away. I lost 40 pounds and my body weight lowered to perfectly normal. When my body resumed normal weight, my obstructive sleep apnea automatically disappeared or reversed perfectly.

As The Day Ends

15. As the day ends by 7 pm or 8 pm, the night begins.
Read below the "Instruction # 16 & Instruction # 17 to understand
what to do as The Night Begins.

DURING THE NIGHT [7 pm to 7 am]

As The Night Begins

16. IT IS IMPORTANT THAT YOU SHOULD PURCHASE A BATTERY-POWERED LAMP. It is available in many dollar-stores for a few bucks.

Battery-Powered Table Lamp, Operates With 3AA Batteries

RCA Swivel LED Lamp
LED=Light-Emitting Diode
I purchased this battery-powered lamp at a Dollar Store for $5.99 when I treated my insomnia in less than a week.

SPECIFICATIONS
12 Super bright white LEDs.
Lifespan of LED bulbs: 100,000 hrs.
Swivel lamp head for directional light.
Operates with 3AA size batteries.
Can be used both indoors and outdoors.

It is capable to illuminate a small room with dim light. It has an ON-OFF button.

Figure 1-3 Battery-powered lamp.

17. DURING THE NIGHT, YOU ESSENTIALLY LIVE IN THE DARK BY STAYING AT HOME (STAY ALWAYS INDOORS) AND DO NOT GO OUT AND DO NOT EXPOSE YOURSELF TO BRIGHT STREET LIGHTS. YOU WOULD USE A BATTERY-POWERED LAMP JUST FOR WALKING FROM PLACE TO PLACE OR FOR DOING SOMETHING WITHIN YOUR HOUSE OR APARTMENT.

As The Night Begins (After The Day Ends), Do the Following:

a. FINISH COOKING & EATING: Finish all cooking and eating by 7 pm. Leave some cooked food in the fridge so that you could eat a little if you get really hungry in the middle of the night. No cooking and no eating dinner after 7 pm. You are essentially going to live in the dark.

b. WEAR PAJAMA AND SLIPPERS: Wear pajama and slippers as the night begins. Prepare to live under darkness after 7 pm as the night approaches. Whenever you wear pajama and slippers, your brain would recognize that it is nighttime, and prepare to produce melatonin from the pineal gland, later in the night. REMEMBER: You are going to wear office clothes and shoes during the daytime. If you develop this habit of wearing the appropriate clothes during the daytime and nighttime, your body and your brain would recognize and distinguish the daytime from nighttime, and will not shut down the melatonin production during the night. Melatonin secretion by pineal gland is the key to maintain sleep throughout the night.

c. TURN OFF ALL CEILING LIGHTS: By 7 pm, you should turn off all the ceiling lights in your house or apartment, and you should use a battery-powered lamp for walking and/or doing something for emergency purposes only. When you are sitting on the couch/sofa, and watching TV (dimmed at low volume), the battery-powered lamp should be turned off. From 7 pm to 7 am, all the lights should be turned off. Do not expose yourself to bright lights howsoever after 7 pm.

d. By 7 pm, turn off the computer, laptop and any other electronics.

e. By 7 pm, turn off your cell phone. Your cell phone should be turned off throughout the night. Do not answer the phone and do not read text messages on the cell phone screen during the nighttime until your chronic insomnia is treated completely and is reversed.

f. CLOSE THE WINDOWS: All the windows should remain closed. You can leave a window partly open for ventilation if you are accustomed to do so.

g. CLOSE THE CURTAINS: All the curtains should be closed making sure no light from outside enters your home. You should live in the **bitter darkness** at least for a few days, especially when you started this insomnia treatment.

h. DO NOT TAKE ANY KIND OF SLEEPING PILLS: Do not take any kind of sleeping pills as your doctor recommends during the night. They are unnecessary and they don't work exactly as they are supposed to. You brain is capable of producing enough melatonin if you let it know exactly when it is daytime and when it is nighttime. ALL YOU GOT TO DO IS: Reset your biological clock located in your brain by living in the dark during the night and by exposure to the sun and bright lights during the day.

i. DIM THE TV SCREEN AND LOWER THE VOLUME DURING THE NIGHT:
Dim the TV screen and lower the volume during the nighttime (7 pm to 7 am).
> You can dim your TV using your TV remote.
> Press menu button, press the brightness button.
> Adjust the brightness to minimum using the arrow buttons.
> Press exit key after you dim the TV.

You can watch TV during the night at low noise. You do the opposite during the daytime (from 7 am to 7 pm), brighten the TV and increase the volume. If you develop this habit, your brain would recognize which is the daytime and which is the nighttime, depending on the brightness of the TV screen and the volume, and produce serotonin and melatonin accordingly.

BY DOING SO, YOU WOULD LET YOUR BRAIN KNOW EXACTLY WHEN THE NIGHTTIME STARTED SO THAT YOUR SUPRACHIASMATIC NECLEUS (SCN) OR MASTER BIOLOGICAL CLOCK WOULD ORDER THE PINEAL GLAND TO PRODUCE APPROPRIATE AMOUNT OF MELATONIN ACCORDINGLY AS THE NIGHT PROGRESSES, AND MAKE YOU SLEEPY THROUGHOUT THE NIGHT.

As The Night Progresses

18. TAKE A HOT BATH BY SOAKING YOURSELF IN THE HOT TUB 90 MINUTES PRIOR TO BEDTIME:

It is the nighttime, and you are essentially living in the darkness in your apartment or house, and all the lights are turned off. You would be using a battery-powered lamp to walk within your living place from one room to the other. At around 8 pm or 9 pm according to your chosen schedule, one or one-and-half hours before going to bed, walk into your bathroom using the battery-powered lamp. Fill the hot tub with hot water, as hot as you could stand and get into your bathtub naked. Creating bubbles in the bathtub could keep the water temperature high for a longer time. You can enhance your hot-water bath efforts by using essential oils and/or the lavender, which acts as a sedative. Turn off the battery-powered lamp while you are soaking in the hot tub. Soak in your bathtub filled with hot water for at least 20 minutes by staying in the dark. The hot bath relaxes your muscles and releases any muscular tension that was built up during the daytime.

Your normal body temperature is 37 °C (98.6 °F). After you soak yourself in hot water for 20 minutes, your body temperature could rise to 39 °C (102 °F). When you finish the hot bath and get out of your bathtub, your body resumes the normal temperature 37 °C (98.6 °F). This sudden body temperature drop from 39 °C (102 °F) to 37 °C (98.6 °F) signals the brain to release melatonin, which tells your body that it is the time to sleep, but melatonin doesn't make you sleepy like a sleeping pill. It is your responsibility to put yourself into the deep sleep mode by relaxing and by living in the dark room. This technique works for some people and they become naturally sleepy after a hot bath.

After you have completed your hot bath, turn on your battery-powered lamp, empty the bathtub and walk out of your bathroom while carrying the lamp with you, and walk in to your living room and then to your bedroom. Then you would wear your nightdress or pajama. Then you should turn off the lamp, go to the bed quickly and try to sleep. If you are not sleepy yet, you can watch TV (dimmed at low volume) for some time, and whenever you start yawning or becomes sleepy, you can walk to the bed, close your eyes and sleep.

However you must always keep in mind that you are essentially living in the dark during the whole night. You would use the battery-powered lamp whenever you need to walk within your apartment/house, and turn off that lamp whenever you are not walking or not doing something.

Figure 1-4 A lady submerged in hot tub (battery-powered lamp is behind her).

19. SLEEP IN A DARK ROOM (PITCH-BLACK ROOM) DURING THE NIGHT:

Sleep in an extremely quiet and dark room (pitch-black room), on a comfortable and cozy bed with nice pillows, throughout the night from 10 pm to 7 am. Wash the bed sheets and pillow-covers once every week or fortnight, and make sure your bedroom and bed are super clean all the time. No noise and no kind of light in the bedroom howsoever.

Figure 1-5 A person sleeping in a dark room at night (pitch-black room).

Figure 1-6 A person sleeping on the side in a dark room at night. Side-sleeping opens your airway, improves your breathing, stops snoring, and helps you sleep better.

20. TRAIN YOURSELF TO SLEEP ON THE SIDE (NOT ON YOUR BACK) [1]

When you sleep on your back, the soft tissue in your throat collapses and blocks the airway, and it is very likely that you could snore. Snoring could block the breathing, and the brain wakes you up frequently whenever your percentage saturation of blood oxygen (SpO2) levels fall more than 4% for more than 10 seconds. If the brain wakes you up too many times, that could become insomnia. You could minimize or completely stop snoring by sleeping on your side, instead of sleeping on your back. Side-sleeping keeps your airway open, stops snoring, and you can then breathe better and sleep better. So train yourself to sleep on your side throughout the night.

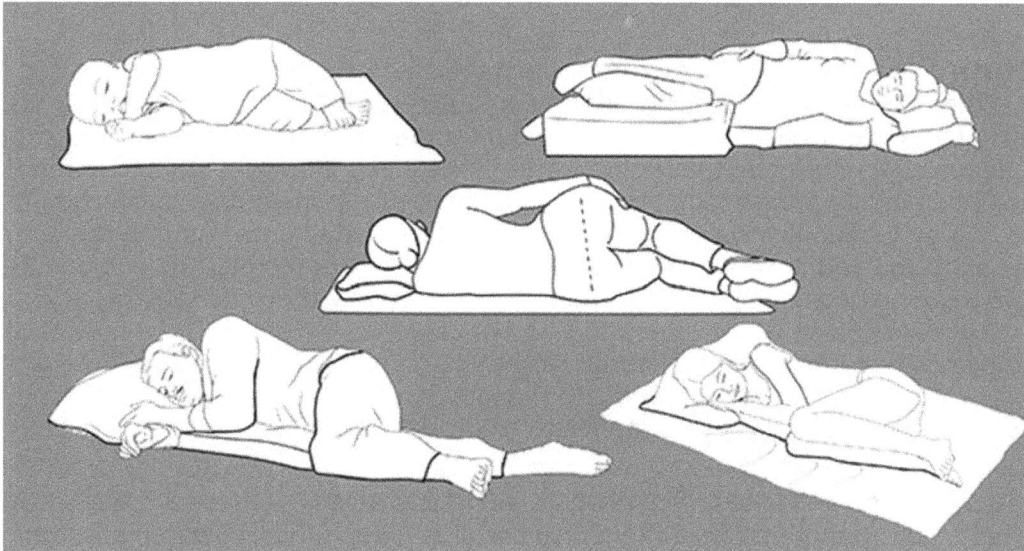

Figure 1-7 Side-sleeping opens your airway, improves your breathing, stops snoring, and helps you sleep better.

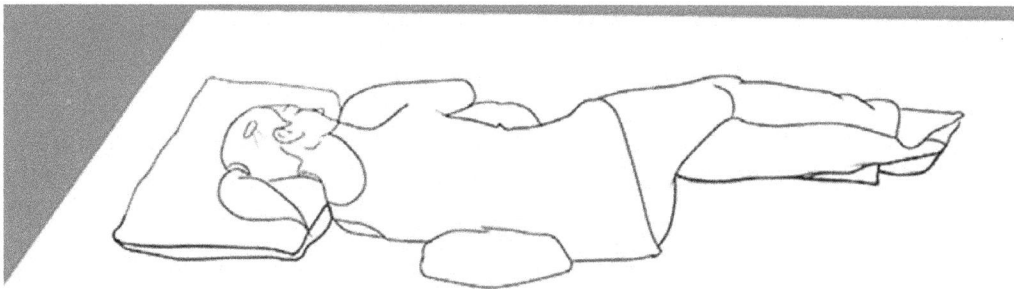

Figure 1-8 Side-sleeping opens your airway, improves your breathing, stops snoring, and helps you sleep better.

21. AVOID DRINKING WATER OR OTHER LIQUIDS AFTER 7 pm:

An adult is supposed to drink at least 8 cups of water per day. Drink all 8 cups during 7 am to 7 pm. After 7 pm, avoid drinking water or other liquids so that your bladder would not be filled with urine during the nighttime when sleeping. If you drink water or other liquids after 7 pm, you may have to wake up too many times for peeing and to empty the bladder, which could disrupt your sleep. However if you are accustomed to drink lots of water during the night, get up for urination, and get back to sleep without facing any insomnia, you can always drink plenty of purified water (RO water or distilled water).

22. SLEEP REMEDIES OR SLEEP AIDS

It is being recommended that you should try to reverse your chronic insomnia without taking any of the following sleep aids being sold in heath food stores, pharmacies OTC, or on the Internet without prescription.

These natural remedies are not guaranteed to work. They work for some people, and may not work for others. They may work for the first time, and don't work every time you use them. It is up to the individual to research on his/her body by trying them in all possible ways to find out if they are beneficial and if they induce sleep whenever needed.

a. Melatonin: Melatonin is a natural hormone produced by the pineal gland located in your brain. When the natural melatonin production depletes due to a sleep disorder, you can supplement it by taking artificial melatonin found over the counter without any prescription. Artificial melatonin is a hormone that helps control your sleep and wake cycles. It can help restore your sleep cycle at least temporarily. Take this artificial melatonin by starting from a low dosage and by gradually increasing the dosage day after day until you find the correct dosage that suits you and makes you sleepy. Also follow the dosage instructions printed on the label. Artificial melatonin liquid drops work more effectively than the tablets.

However it is known that artificial melatonin works when you try it for the first time or take it occasionally, but may not work if you use it repeatedly every day for an extended period of time because your body creates resistance to artificial melatonin.

b. Valarian, Hops, Passion Flower & White Zapote: These are the sedative herbal extracts that promote sleep. Take a dropperful in a cup of warm water or soothing organic herbal tea that is caffeine-free. [2]

c. Kava: Kava is a herb from the South Pacific known to help relax tense muscles. Kava was also found to be an excellent herb for relieving anxiety. Take a 200 mg dose of Kava extract standardized to 70 mg of Kava lactones. [2]

d. Calcium Citrate: Take a 600 mg of tablet or softgel about 45 minutes before going to bed. Calcium citrate is highly absorbable by the body. Calcium is primarily involved in slowing nerve transmission and in muscle relaxation. In other words, it has a sedative effect upon the nervous and muscular systems. [3]

e. Magnesium Citrate: Take a 300 mg of tablet or softgel about 45 minutes before going to bed. Magnesium citrate is highly absorbable by the body. Magnesium is an antidote to stress and a powerful relaxation mineral. Magnesium helps to relax muscles, relieves muscle aches and spasms, calms nerves, helps you fall asleep and treats insomnia. [4]

As The Night Ends

23. As the night ends by 6 am, 7 am or 8 am, the day begins.
Go to the "Instruction # 10 As the Day Begins," and read through to understand what to do as The Day Begins. As The Night Ends, The Day Begins.

24. HOW TO TREAT THE MIDDLE-OF-THE-NIGHT INSOMNIA

Please read through CHAPTER 4 for a detailed discussion on Middle-of-the-Night Insomnia.

Research proved that Middle-of-the-Night Insomnia is a very common and normal sleep pattern, and should not be considered a sleep disorder. So do not panic too much and deal with it by exercising calmness and patience. There is nothing to worry, our ancestors used to experience middle-of-the-night insomnia, and used to sleep in two phases every night. Sleep for 4 hours, remain awake for one to two hours in the middle of the night, and sleep again till the morning for another 4 hours. It is called segmented sleep, and is explained in detail in CHAPTER 4.

TIPS TO TREAT AND COMBAT MIDDLE-OF-THE-NIGHT INSOMNIA:

DO SOME OR ALL OF THE FOLLOWING TASKS WHENEVER YOU ARE ATTACKED BY MIDDLE-OF-THE-NIGHT INSOMNIA:

(i) MAINTAIN A REGULAR CONSISTENT SLEEP SCHEDULE AND MAKE SURE YOU ARE SLEEPING ON A COMFORTABLE BED AND PILLOWS: Go to bed at 9 pm or 10 pm and get up by 7 am or 8 am every day. Stick to this schedule and do not change it no matter what happens. Make sure your bedroom, bed and pillows are comfortable, clean and quiet. There should not be any noise howsoever during the nighttime. Invest some money in purchasing a nice bed and pillows. Always sleep on your side (not on the back), which would keep your airway open and minimize the snoring.

(ii) GET OUT OF YOUR BED AND DO SOMETHING IN THE DARK IF YOU ARE ATTACKED BY MIDDLE-OF-THE-NIGHT INSOMNIA: If you are wide awake and fully alert, tossing and turning, and unable to get back to sleep for more than 20 minutes, you should get out of the bed, and walk to the living room and sit on the couch/sofa for a while. It is important that you are sitting in the dark without any light.

IMPORTANT NOTE: Relax and do not panic, and focus on your breath. Do not let negative thoughts or past experiences come to your mind. Just think about the present moment. Breathe in, hold and breathe out. Focus on meditation so that all the thoughts are diminished. Or say some silent prayer, and repeat the same prayer over and over again, and focus on your prayer forgetting everything around you all the time until you become sleepy. Even if you are an atheist, you can meditate and say a prayer to nothingness or higher power. When you are really sleepy or find yourself yawning, go back to the bed and sleep. Or you can do all of the above while lying on the bed. When you are sleepy, you sleep on your side. Side-sleeping keeps your airway open and stops snoring so you can breathe better and sleep longer.

(iii) ALWAYS USE A BATTERY-POWERED LAMP FOR WALKING WITHIN THE HOUSE OR APARTMENT: Never turn on the ceiling lights during night from 7 pm to 7 am even if you are attacked by the middle-of-the-night insomnia. Stay in the dark throughout the night. Use the battery-powered lamp to walk to your living room, kitchen or bathroom. Do not leave the battery-powered lamp turned on for a long time. Use it only when you are walking from place to place and doing something in the kitchen or bathroom, and turn the lamp off when you get back to your bed or couch.

Leave the lamp on the countertop far away from you, and avoid looking at the lamp (You are using the lamp just for visibility). You can even watch TV (dimmed, at low volume) until you become really sleepy. When you become really sleepy or when you are yawning, go back to the bed and sleep.

(iv) PRACTICE RELAXATION MEDITATION: If you are attacked by Middle-of-the-Night Insomnia, get up and walk to the living room, sit with your computer desk, and practice relaxation meditation by sitting in the dark. Listen to binaural music for sleeping. There are many free videos on YouTube. Try the following video: https://www.youtube.com/watch?v=afEo2rxXAoM

When you have turned on the computer or laptop, and started the audio to listen to the binaural music (audio only), do not look at the monitor screen. Cover the monitor screen with a towel or cloth. When you are listening to the binaural music, focus on your breath. Breathe in, hold and breathe out. Focus on meditating so that all thoughts are diminished.

When you practice this kind of meditation, your beta state of mind would quickly switch to alpha state of mind, and your brainwave frequencies slow down. Meditation keeps your busy thoughts from intruding, and you become calm and drowsy. When you are really sleepy or find yourself yawning, turn off the binaural music, and go back to the bed and sleep.

(v) TAKE A HOT BATH BY SOAKING YOURSELF IN A HOT TUB 90 MINUTES BEFORE BEDTIME: If you are attacked by Middle-of-the-Night Insomnia, get up and walk to the bathroom, and take a hot bath in the dark bathroom (as explained above). Use the battery-powered lamp only to get into the bathroom and fill the bathtub with hot water, and turn off the lamp while you are soaking in the tub for 20 minutes. A sudden body temperature drop after the hot bath should put you in sleep mode. Your normal body temperature is 37 °C (98.6 °F). After you soak yourself in hot water for 20 minutes, your body temperature could rise to 39 °C (102 °F). When you finish the hot bath and get out of your bathtub, your body resumes the normal temperature 37 °C (98.6 °F). This sudden body temperature drop from 39 °C (102 °F) to 37 °C (98.6 °F) signals the brain to release melatonin, which tells your body that it is the time to sleep. When you are really sleepy or find yourself yawning, go back to the bed and sleep.

(vi) DRINK SOME WARM ORGANIC MILK WITH ORGANIC HONEY: If you are attacked by Middle-of-the-Night Insomnia, and if you are still not able to sleep, turn on your battery-powered lamp again, walk to the kitchen, drink a cup of warm organic skim milk or 1% milk with organic honey. Organic honey is soothing. Avoid honey if you are diabetic or inject the appropriate amount of insulin if you want honey. Milk contains L-tryptophan, an amino acid and precursor of both serotonin and melatonin, both of which promote sleep. Calcium present in the milk also helps you relax better. Get back to your couch/sofa, turn off the lamp, sit there and relax for some time. Focus on your breath. Breathe in, hold and breathe out. Let all thoughts be diminished. When you are really sleepy or find yourself yawning, go back to the bed and sleep.

(vii) EAT SOME LOW-CALORIE AND LOW-FAT SALAD WITH COTTAGE CHEESE AND DRINK A CUP OF ICE-COLD WATER: If you are attacked by Middle-of-the-Night Insomnia, and if you are still not able to sleep, turn on your battery-powered lamp again, walk to the kitchen, grab some low-calorie salads or fruits and cottage cheese (it is high in protein), drink a large cup of ice-cold water, and walk to your living room, turn off the battery-powered lamp, and spend some time on your couch/sofa by staying in the dark until you really feel like falling asleep. Be always in a relaxed mood, and don't think about your past experiences. All thoughts should be diminished. Breathe in, hold and breathe out. Just think about the present. When you are really sleepy or find yourself yawning, go back to bed and sleep.

(viii) READ A BOOK UNDER THE THE BATTERY-POWERED LAMP USING BLUE-LIGHT BLOCKING GLASSES: Blue light from the bright lights impedes your body's ability to fall asleep naturally because it interferes with the natural production of melatonin from your pineal gland located in your brain.

If you are still not sleepy after taking warm milk and after eating some low-calories food, and after meditating, read a health book or non-fiction book under the the battery-powered lamp by wearing **blue-light blocking glasses**. You can purchase blue-light blocking glasses on Amazon. When you are really sleepy or find yourself yawning, go back to the bed in the pitch-black dark room, just forget yourself, relax, and fall into sleep.

Figure 1.9 Blue-light blocking glasses (available on Amazon).

(ix) BONUS READING FROM CHAPTER 4
Middle-of-the-Night Insomnia Could Be A Normal Sleep Pattern

Don't panic if you can't sleep continuously for 8 hours (like you used to sleep when you were a child). You can divide the total length of your sleep into several segments, add those segments you have slept, and in average if you slept 7 to 8 hours a day, you should be happy.

SEGMENTED SLEEP: Segmented sleep, also known as divided sleep or interrupted sleep, is a sleep pattern where two or more periods of sleep are punctuated by a period of wakefulness. Along with a nap/siesta in the day, it has been argued that this in fact is the natural pattern of human sleep and helps to regulate stress.

During 1990s, an American psychiatrist Dr. Thomas Wehr conducted a study on photoperiodicity in humans to understand the sleep-wake cycle. He selected 8 healthy sleepers (8 healthy men) who were not troubled with insomnia at that time and who were accustomed to live in 16 to 17 hours of daytime and 8 or 7 hours of nighttime for sleep.

He placed them in a strictly organized quiet room. All 8 sleepers developed a sleep pattern characterized by two sleep sessions in two phases or two segments: All 8 subjects, when they were exposed to dark, tended to lie awake for 1 to 2 hours, and then fall quickly asleep. After about 4 hours of solid sleep, they would remain awake and spend 1 to 2 hours in a state of quiet wakefulness, experiencing some sort of INSOMNIA, and then they slept for another 4 hours. Which means they slept in two segments: 4 hours in the first segment and another 4 hours in the second segment. Dr. Wehr also observed that there was a spike in their melatonin levels during the phase-II sleep or second segment.

INSTRUCTION # 25
Light Therapy For Seasonal Affective Disorder (SAD) & Winter Blues

When you become unable to treat your insomnia by using the aforementioned 24 instructions, then you consider understanding and implementing Instruction # 25 as explained below.

Winter Blues
⦿ In some regions around the globe, during the winter months, Sun disappears emitting no sunshine. Daytime could be shorter and night time could be longer. During this winter time, when sunshine is not available, the production of both serotonin and melatonin in your body is depleted, thereby developing either winter blues or seasonal affective disorder (SAD). Winter blues occurs in winter months causing sadness, mood change, lack of interest in performing daily activities, mild depression and also insomnia during the night. Winter blues can be treated with lifestyle changes with or without using any light therapy.

Seasonal Affective Disorder (SAD)
⦿ Whereas Seasonal Affective Disorder (SAD) occurs in both winter and summer months causing depression, insomnia and even chronic insomnia.
⦿ If you suffer from SAD, you may feel the symptoms such as sadness, grumpy, moody, or anxious. You may lose interest in your usual activities, and don't feel like working at all. You may gain weight as you don't sleep sufficient number of hours during the night. SAD can be treated with light therapy as explained below.

TREATMENT OF SAD USING LIGHT THERAPY
⦿ LIGHT THERAPY needs a light therapy box or a lamp which can be easily plugged into the power outlet at your home, and can be turned on or off. The machine is built with either fluorescent lamps or LED lamps. LED lamps last forever and you don't need replacement bulbs. If the machine is built with fluorescent lamps, you will have to replace the lamps once every few years after they are burned out.
⦿ Light therapy lamps are manufactured covering with a plastic screen to diffuse the light and to filter out harmful ultraviolet rays. So you don't have to worry about ultraviolet radiations that could damage your eyes.
⦿ Light therapy lamps are manufactured to emit the light with a luminosity of 10,000 lux. You should sit close to your light box by maintaining 16 to 24 inches from your face for about 30 minutes every morning within one hour after you wake up. While sitting with the light box, do not look at the lamp directly but you should keep your eyes always open so that your retinas receive light with a luminosity of 10,000 lux, and signals your brain to produce serotonin.
⦿ The light therapy machine is designed to emit a bright light that mimics and simulates outdoor sunshine, boosting serotonin, melatonin and vitamin D. Serotonin is produced in the skin, gut and brain and helps regulate the immune and vascular systems of the skin. The pineal gland of your brain makes melatonin during the night using some of the serotonin. If there is no serotonin available in your body, no melatonin is produced causing insomnia (no melatonin means no sleep).
⦿ You should sit with the light box by maintaining the same schedule every morning. You can extend the timer longer than one hour, especially at night or on cloudy days. Please read and follow all instructions in the manual provided by the manufacturer.

CAREX Day Light Classic Plus Lamp to Treat SAD

The wider the screen of the lamp, the more light it emits to your face and body, and more effective the light therapy could be. Sit in front of the light box for 30 minutes every morning within one hour after you wake up. Remove your shirt and expose your entire upper body to the light therapy lamp. Do not look at the lamp but keep your eyes open. And maintain a distance of 16 to 24 inches from your face (follow the manufacturer's instructions).

Carex day light classic plus lamp is being recommended for best results. Please visit the following websites, do your own research, and purchase a lamp that suits your condition.

US Websites
https://carex.com/
https://www.day-lights.com/

Canadian Website (Resellers)
https://www.halohealthcare.com/
https://www.halohealthcare.com/carex-sunlite-therapy-light/

Sunlight & SAD Explained Here
https://carex.com/blogs/resources/light-deprivation-what-happens-if-you-don-t-get-enough-sunlight

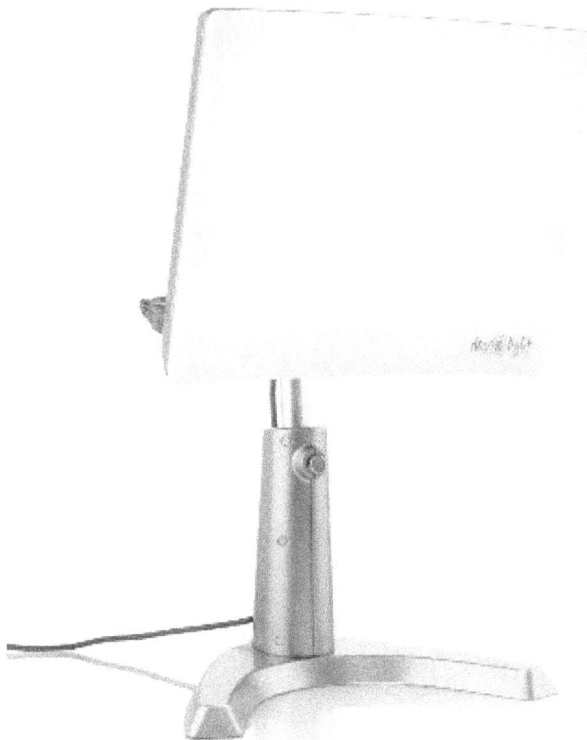

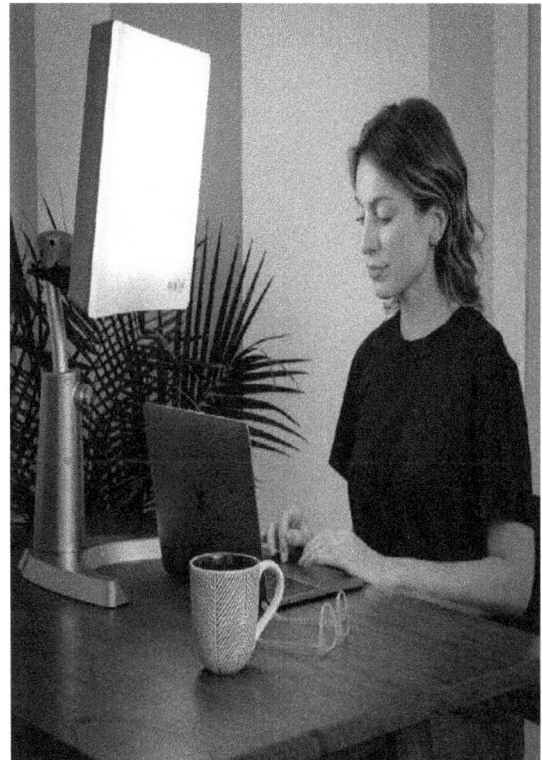

Figure 1.10 CAREX Day Light Classic Plus Lamp to Treat Seasonal Affective Disorder (SAD). Courtesy of Carex.

MEDICAL CONDITIONS THAT IMPEDE THE INSOMNIA TREATMENT

(i) CONTINUE TAKING ALL MEDICATIONS AND SUPPLEMENTS AS USUAL

Please do not discontinue your medications and supplements during this insomnia treatment. Continue taking all medications and supplements as usual.

(ii) VITAMIN-D DEFICIENCY IMPEDES INSOMNIA TREATMENT [5]

Research has showed that there is a link between poor sleep and Vitamin-D deficiency. Do a blood test and make certain that your Vitamin-D level is in the optimal range (over 100 nmol/L).
Blood Test to Be Performed: 25-HydroxiVitamin-D

RESULT		
	75 – 150 nmol/L	Normal Range
	< 25 nmol/L	Deficient
	25 - 74 nmol/L	Insufficient
	75-199 nmol/L	Sufficient
	> 200 nmol/L	Toxic

The exposure to the sunlight every day for 30 minutes to an hour would boost your Vitamin-D level naturally. If your Vitamin-D level is below 100, take some over the counter Vitamin-D softgels or liquid drops so that your Vitamin-D level is in the optimal range (over 100 nmol/L).

(iii) HYPOTHYROIDISM OR HYPERTHYROIDISM COULD ALSO IMPEDE YOUR ATTEMPTS TO REVERSE CHRONIC INSOMNIA [6, 7]

If your thyroid is not functioning properly, your body's chemistry would get out of balance, affecting circadian rhythm. Your master biological clock that is responsible for your sleep-wake cycle will eventually be disturbed, causing a sleep disorder called insomnia.

Two of the major thyroid dysfunctional problems are: (i) Hypothryroidism or underactive thyroid function and (ii) Hyperthyroidism or overactive thyroid dysfunction.
If you have hypothyroidism or underactive thyroid function, inadequate thyroid hormones are secreted by the thyroid gland, and as result some people may experience upper airway obstruction that leads to difficulties in breathing during sleep, developing both obstructive sleep apnea and insomnia. Hypothyroidism is usually treated with prescription medications such as Synthroid, Armour / Desiccated Thyroid / ERFA Thyroid Tabs, Cytomel or other.

On the other hand, if you have hyperthyroidism or overactive thyroid dysfunction, too much thyroid hormones are secreted by the thyroid gland, resulting in hyperfunctioning thyroid goiter, Graves' disease, or thyroiditis. This problem is usually treated with radioactive iodine. Several studies indicated that hyperthyroidism could also cause insomnia in some people.

If you are seriously suffering from chronic insomnia, you should also check your thyroid function by doing a blood test for TSH, Free T4 and Free T3 and should make sure that the test results are normal. If these test results are not normal, you should take the appropriate steps to fix your thyroid problem before trying to reverse chronic insomnia.

(iv) ELEVATED CORTISOL LEVELS COULD ALSO IMPEDE YOUR ATTEMPTS TO REVERSE CHRONIC INSOMNIA [8, 9]

A typical INSOMNIAC has elevated cortisol level, and cannot fall asleep or stay asleep and may stay in a state of arousal 24 hours a day. This can result in chronic insomnia. Even if an INSOMNIAC sleeps a few hours a day, that could be a very light sleep and is not at all refreshing. Some INSOMNIACS get used to segmented sleep. It may happen if you are living in a consistent state of stress, anxiety, and some health-related issues. Elevated cortisol levels impede your attempts to treat and reverse chronic insomnia.

Please do a blood test for AM Cortisol and PM cortisol, find out what was going on with your cortisol levels, and make sure that the results are normal.

> The AM blood collection should be done between 7am and 9am.
> The PM blood collection should be done between 3pm and 5pm.

You can take a natural supplement to treat your high cortisol levels. However you must fix your elevated cortisol level before trying to reverse your chronic insomnia.

(v) ATTENTION WOMEN! YOUR ABNORMAL ESTROGEN OR PROGESTERONE LEVEL COULD ALSO IMPEDES YOUR ATTEMPTS TO REVERSE CHRONIC INSOMNIA: [10]

When a woman reaches the menopause phase, the ovaries begin producing lesser amounts of key hormones such as estrogen and progesterone. As these hormone levels fall, symptoms of menopause show up, one of which is insomnia.

If you are being attacked by Middle-of-the-Night Insomnia frequently, it is likely that you are suffering from estrogen/progesterone imbalance. Do a blood test or saliva test or both for hormonal imbalance, and take appropriate steps to correct this imbalance so that you will be able to treat and reverse your chronic insomnia, and sleep well thereafter.

(vi) NUTRITIONAL DEFICIENCY AND MINERAL DEFICIENCY

Obviously any kind of nutritional or mineral deficiency could definitely impact your general health and sleep patterns, and may impede your attempts to treat or reverse your chronic insomnia. Please do a blood test to find out if you are deficient in certain essential and most common nutrients such as Iron (ferritin), Vitamin B12, Vitamin D, calcium, magnesium, potassium, phosphate and sodium. If any of these tests are not normal, you should treat and fix that deficiency by taking the appropriate high-quality supplement.

(vii) IF YOU ARE DIABETIC, CONTROL YOUR DIABETES PERMANENTLY [11]

If you are diabetic, you must make sure that your diabetes is perfectly controlled. Take the following blood tests once every 3 months, and make certain that all tests are normal. If any test is not normal, you should take the appropriate medications and/or supplements so that all tests would be within the normal range.

TESTS TO BE PERFORMED IF YOU ARE DIABETIC: Fasting Glucose, Hemoglobin A1c, Cholesterol Tests (total cholesterol, HDL and LDL), Triglycerides, Thyroid Test (TSH, Free T4 and Free T3), Prostate Test (PSA), Urine Test, Kidney Test, and Liver Test. If you are on cholesterol-lowering statin drug, you must take liver test once every 3 months.
If you are diabetic, please visit www.mydiabetescontrol.com, and learn how to control your diabetes in 90 days, and learn how to live like a normal person for the rest of your life.

(viii) CHECK IF YOU HAVE SLEEP APNEA [1]

Check yourself if you have sleep apnea by taking the "Overnight Pulse Oximetry Test." You can have a free test from any CPAP vendor in your area. If you have sleep apnea, you should sleep with a CPAP or mouthpiece or it could largely contribute to chronic insomnia. By losing weight, it is possible to reverse obstructive sleep apnea. So you should work hard to reverse insomnia. Or as long as you sleep with the CPAP machine, you should be able to live like a normal person, and sleep well. Please visit www.reversingsleepapnea.com, and learn how to reverse obstructive sleep apnea.

(ix) DO YOU HAVE CHRONIC PAIN, ARTHRITIS, FIBROMYALGIA OR MUSCLE TENSION?

If you have chronic pain developed due to arthritis, fibromyalgia or other muscle tension, it could also cause insomnia and impedes your attempts to reverse insomnia. So you should fix the chronic pain problem first in order to treat and reverse your chronic insomnia.

COFFEEINE CONSUMPTION GUIDELINES (by Dr. RK)
BONUS READING (Summary of Chapter 7)

● **Limited caffeine consumption has positive effects**. Each person is different! So each person must determine optimum number of cups of coffee (how many cups of coffee per day) by trial and error, and must drink all that coffee before noon.

● **Overconsumption of caffeine disrupts sleep, causes chronic insomnia, chronic pain, fatigue and other health issues**. Anxiety, insomnia, muscle aches, PMS (premenstrual syndrome), headaches, heartburn, and irritability are the other common symptoms.

● You should always keep an eye on every food item and drink you consume in restaurants and coffee-shops, as most drinks and some foods contain caffeine. For example, Coke, Diet Coke, Pepsi, Diet Pepsi and other soft drinks contain a lot of caffeine. Beware of the foods and drinks that contain elevated levels of caffeine, and keep them in your block list. Be cautious about caffeine content whenever you eat and drink out.

● Please do not take coffee or decaf in restaurants as the caffeine content there could be dangerously high. For example, Americano is loaded with too much caffeine. Do your own research and drink coffee or decaf at home.

● Research and find out exactly how much caffeine is present per cup of that selected volume of coffee you aimed to drink. Know exactly how much caffeine you consume per day by doing some reasonable calculations and by checking the labels of the coffee you purchased. If you do so, you can easily control the amount of caffeine being consumed per day, and can take action if you are affected by overconsumption.

● If you are too sensitive to caffeine, more particularly if you are over 55 years old with underlying health conditions, you better make your coffee at home from organic ground coffee powder. Stick to the same brand, stick to the same schedule and plan ahead by consuming optimal number of cups of coffee (1 cup, 2 cups or 3 cups per day to be determined by trial and error).

● Under critical circumstances, quitting coffee would be a great idea at least for some time. You can always get back to consuming limited coffee again. Withdrawal symptoms would last a few days, and it is not that difficult to quit coffee drinking. Try it out, you quit coffee for some time and you can re-start it anytime if needed. For example if you are too sleepy during the day, you need to re-introduce coffee or decaf again to keep you alert. Your own research would guide you and help you cure your insomnia and save your life.

● **Instead of quitting coffee, you can consume "Decaf Coffee" to avoid withdrawal symptoms**.
♦ Please note that decaf is not 100% free of caffeine. The decaffeination process does not allow to remove more than 97% of the caffeine, meaning that at least 3% of caffeine is still present in decaf coffee (in some brands, it could be a lot more than 3% of caffeine).

♦ So "Decaf Coffee" presents an opportunity for you to consume a tiny or very limited amount of caffeine that could help keep you alert during the day. However consume all that decaf your body needs before noon, and do not consume any coffee or decaf after noon.

CAFFEINE ALTERNATIVES

All kinds of coffee and any regular tea, including green tea, contain caffeine. However herbal tea does not contain caffeine. The following products are available in many heath food stores as alternatives to coffee. All these products, also called herbal coffees, contain chicory, which has some adverse side effects. They don't taste as good as some people say. It is up to the each individual to try and find out if any of these products can be used as an alternative to coffee drinking. You can purchase the following products in a local health food store. You can also try to find them on Amazon or by doing Google search.

1. Teeccino Caffe, Inc
    Santa Barbara, CA-93140
    Toll Free: 1-800-493-3434
    http://teeccino.com/

2. ALKAVA
    7298 Hume Avenue,
    Delta, BC, Canada, V4G 1C5
    Ph: 604-946-7277
    https://www.londondrugs.com/

3. Dandy Blend
    P.O.Box 446
    Valley City, Ohio 44280
    http://www.dandyblend.com/

4. Pero All Natural Beverage Coffee Substitute
    1455 Broad Street, 4th Floor
    Bloomfield, NJ 07003
    Phone: 973-338-1499
    https://worldfiner.com/

5. Organic Rooibas Red Tea (Herbal Tea, Containing No Caffeine), preferably taken with organic skim milk or 1% milk. It is being recommended as the best alternative to coffee drinking. It tastes good, gives energy, and you would be easily accustomed to it within a week after quitting coffee. Try It Out!

ENJOY ROOIBOS TEA.

Figure 1.10 Rooibas red tea (100% certified organic herbal tea).

Rooibas Red Tea (100% Certified Organic Herbal Tea)
Best Caffeine Alternative (Milk Tea) Being Recommended!

Courtesy of Swanson Vitamins
Rooibos Red Tea is available at www.swansonvitamins.com
Rooibos Red Tea (100% Certified Organic), Item # SWF082, 20 Bags, $3.99
https://www.swansonvitamins.com/swanson-organic-certified-organic-rooibos-red-tea-20-bags-s

Rooibas Chai (Herbal Tea + Hot Water + Hot Milk + Cardamom)

Cardamom Pods and Seeds

PREPARATION OF MILK HERBAL TEA/CHAI (Alternative to Coffee)
1. Boil purified water (do not drink tap water) using an electric kettle.
2. Add one-quarter cup of organic skim milk or 1% milk to a mug, and microwave it for 1 minute.
3. Place two or three bags of Organic Rooibas Red Tea/Ginger Tea/Other Organic Herbal Tea in the mug that contained one-quarter cup of hot organic skim milk or 1% milk.
4. Pour boiled water into the mug until it is full, and allow the tea from tea-bags to dissolve in the mug. You can press the tea bags to the wall of the mug by using a spoon. You will see the golden-brown color or chai color of herbal tea made from hot water and milk, as shown in the picture above.
5. Break cardamom pods with a knife and remove the seeds and add both skin and seeds to the hot tea in the mug, you will sense a delicious aroma and flavor while drinking the tea. Cardamom pods and seeds can be chewed as a breath freshener. Cardamom has many health benefits. Both the seeds and pod give a pleasant aroma and flavor. Enjoy the Chai!

Figure 1.11 Chai made from organic Rooibas red tea, hot water, hot milk & cardamom.

SUMMARY OF INSOMNIA TREATMENT

DURING THE DAY	DURING THE NIGHT
◐ DURING THE DAY, YOU ESSENTIALLY LIVE UNDER SUNLIGHT WHENEVER YOU ARE OUTDOORS OR UNDER BRIGHT LIGHTS WHENEVER YOU ARE INDOORS. ◐ BY DOING SO, YOU WOULD LET YOUR BRAIN KNOW EXACTLY WHICH HOURS ARE THE DAY (For example 6 am to 6 pm or 7 am to 7 pm or 8 am to 8 pm). Each person is different so you can choose your DAY hours.	◐ DURING THE NIGHT, YOU ESSENTIALLY LIVE IN THE DARK BY STAYING AT HOME (ALWAYS STAY INDOORS) AND DO NOT GO OUTSIDE AND DO NOT EXPOSE YOURSELF TO BRIGHT LIGHTS. ◐ BY DOING SO, YOU WOULD LET YOUR BRAIN KNOW EXACTLY WHICH HOURS ARE THE NIGHT (For example 6 pm to 6 am or 7 pm to 7 am or 8 pm to 8 am). Each person is different so you can choose your NIGHT hours.

IMPORTANT NOTES

● Be persistent, and do not give up after trying it out tentatively for a few days. Focus on the treatment, and try it out seriously, for at least a few weeks, by exposing yourself to the sun or bright lights during the day, and by living strictly in a dark place during the night after 7 pm. You will be successful in reversing your insomnia if you try it seriously!

● After reversing your chronic insomnia, you can live with your family, but all members should follow the rules for the rest of your life. BE CAREFUL! If you get back to exposing to bright lights during the nighttime, you may experience chronic insomnia again. So maintain strict rules during the nighttime, do not expose to the bright lights after 7 pm. If you live like that, you should be able sleep like a baby for the rest of your life.

SLEEP HYGIENE (General Guidelines)

Sleep hygiene is a variety of different practices and habits, a person implements by exercising high willpower and high self-discipline, that are necessary to have good night's sleep and full daytime alertness.

You Can Improve Your Sleep Hygiene and Can Reverse Insomnia:

● by exposing to the sun and/or by living under the bright lights during the daytime, and by living in the pitch-black darkness (always indoors) during the nighttime from 7 pm to 7 am. Watching TV (dimmed at low volume) is okay.
● by using a battery-powered lamp during night to walk within the house or apartment.
● by avoiding coffee, nicotine and alcohol consumption for life. Decaf or herbal tea is okay.
● by quitting all caffeine-containing foods and drinks.
● by taking organic herbal tea (which has no caffeine) with milk as a coffee substitute.
● by managing consistent and fixed schedule for going to bed and for waking up.
● by maintaining a quiet, clean and comfortable sleeping room (nice bed and nice pillows).
● by avoiding napping during the day (no naps between 7 am and 7 pm).
● by exercising every day and by avoiding the exercise within 4 hours of bedtime.
● by avoiding eating a heavy meal late at night (eating a light meal is okay).

INSOMNIA TREATMENT: How Long?

PLEASE REVIEW ALL 24 INSTRUCTIONS CAREFULLY!
AND GRASP ALL CONCEPTS OUTLINED IN THIS CHAPTER!

● If you read, understand and follow all the aforementioned 24 instructions carefully and responsibly, and if you exercise high willpower and high self-discipline without breaking the aforementioned rules, you should be able to reverse insomnia within a week. It is very possible to reverse insomnia in 3 days if you follow the instructions rigorously. Yes, Dr. RK reversed his chronic insomnia in 3 days after suffering from it for more than 3 years.

● Each person reacts differently to the aforementioned insomnia treatment. Living strictly in a pitch-black dark and quiet place during the nighttime is of extreme importance to treat chronic insomnia. Living alone during this treatment period could greatly enhance your ability to reverse chronic insomnia, as there would be nobody to disturb you. Do not expose to the bright lights under any circumstances during the night between 7 pm and 7 am. Use a battery-powered lamp only when walking within your house or apartment.

REFERENCES

1. Reversing Sleep Apnea: Proof that Sleep Apnea Can Be Reversed By Losing Weight!, Authored by Rao Konduru, PhD, April 19, 2018, www.ReversingSleepApnea.com

2. Caffeine Blues: Wake Up to the Hidden Dangers of America's #1 Drug by Stephen Cherniske, MS, ISBN # 0446673919, Book Published by Warner Books, New York, 1998, Pages 369-373.

3. Calcium by Dr. Dr. Lawrence Wilson.
http://drlwilson.com/Articles/calcium.htm

4. Should You Be Taking Magnesium Supplements? by Dr. Axe.
https://draxe.com/magnesium-supplements/

5. A vitamin D deficiency might affect your sleep. Here's what you need to know by Arielle Tschinkel, Insider.com, Posted on Feb 1, 2019.
https://www.insider.com/how-vitamin-d-affects-sleep-2019-2

6. Can Your Thyroid Gland and Thyroid Hormones Cause Sleep Disorders? by Brandon Peters, MD, Medically Reviewed by Elizabeth Molina Ortiz, MD, MPH, Verywell Health.com, Posted on March 03, 2020.
https://www.verywellhealth.com/thyroid-hormones-sleep-disorders-3014705

7. Thyroid Problems and Insomnia by Jon Cooper, Medically Reviewed by Michael W. Smith, MD, WebMD, Posted on July 15, 2021.
https://www.webmd.com/sleep-disorders/thyroid-and-insomnia

8. High Cortisol May be Causing Your Insomnia by Martin Reed, Patient Advocate, HealthCentra.com, Posted on April 22, 2015.
https://www.healthcentral.com/article/high-cortisol-may-be-causing-your-insomnia

9. Cortisol and its Effects on Your Sleep by Dr. Michael Breus, Posted on March 24, 2020.
https://thesleepdoctor.com/2020/03/24/cortisol-and-its-effects-on-your-sleep/

10. Can Menopause Cause Insomnia? by Kimberly Holland, Medically reviewed by Stacy A. Henigsman, DO, Posted and Updated on August 9, 2021.
https://www.healthline.com/health/menopause/menopause-and-insomnia#takeaway

11. Permanent Diabetes Control (book), Authored by Rao Konduru, MS, PhD, DSc, Reviewed and Endorsed by Dr. Marshall Dahl, MD, PhD, Faculty of Medicine, University of British Columbia, Canada, First Published in 2003, Revised and Rewritten in 2021, www.mydiabetescontrol.com

ATTENTION READERS: There Are 2 Books!
Both books are revised and rewritten in 2021.

BOOK # 1: Reversing Insomnia
It is the complete book with all 7 Chapters, 180 Pages, 32 Figures and 7 Tables.
Insomnia Treatment is explained in Chapter 1.

BOOK # 2: Reversing Insomnia in 3 Days
It is Chapter 1 only, 52 Pages and 10 Figures.
Insomnia Treatment is explained in Chapter 1.

However both books teach "Insomnia Treatment" in Chapter 1.

If you want to read all 7 chapters, please purchase "REVERSING INSOMNIA," ISBN # 9780973112016.

TABLE OF CONTENTS: REVERSING INSOMNIA

Limited Caffeine Consumption Has Positive Effects!
Overconsumption of Caffeine Has Negative Effects!
Overconsumption of Caffeine Causes Chronic Insomnia, Chronic Pain & Chronic Fatigue!

TABLE OF CONTENTS

About the Author

Dr. Rao M Konduru was a Chemical Engineer, and held two Master's degrees and two doctorates and two post-doctoral titles, all in chemical engineering. He published a book in 2003 titled "Permanent Diabetes Control," which earned immense respect and appreciation. Many people said it was a wonderful book. After suffering from a sudden heart attack in 1998, even though his left artery was 75% clogged with severe angina, he said "NO" to bypass surgery. He did what none of us would even think of doing. He simply relied on his natural self-prevention diet and exercise, and with it he reversed his critical diabetic heart disease in a matter of months, and developed a method to accomplish Permanent Diabetes Control. He also came up with a trial-and-error procedure to determine the optimal insulin dose that would tightly control diabetes, and would allow a diabetic person to live like a normal person for the rest of his/her life.

Dr. Rao M Konduru maintained his hemoglobin A1c level under 6.0% consistently. His personal best hemoglobin A1c level of 5.0% was an extraordinary result any diabetic person would hope to accomplish in a lifetime. Perhaps Dr. Rao M Konduru was the only diabetic person lived in this world with "Permanent Diabetes Control".

Once again, health demons such as uncontrollable weight gain, sleep apnea and chronic insomnia came his way. He did not give up, but persisted on discovering new, natural and effortless treatments of his own in reversing these most difficult disorders. His extensive scientific research experience and his powerful knowledge helped him battle and combat these life challenges. He figured out their root causes, and developed natural yet powerful techniques to cure these health disorders himself. After losing 40 pounds of weight and 12 inches around the waist, he successfully reversed his obesity, obstructive sleep apnea and chronic insomnia. He carefully created and published the following excellent guidebooks on Amazon so that others can benefit and be inspired to achieve similar results. His most recent book "Drinking Water Guide" is a 540-page book of wealth of information on drinking water for the rest of us.

1. Permanent Diabetes Control — www.mydiabetescontrol.com
2. The Secret to Controlling Type 2 Diabetes — www.mydiabetescontrol.com
3. Reversing Obesity — www.reversingsleepapnea.com/ebook2.html
4. Reversing Sleep Apnea — www.reversingsleepapnea.com
5. Reversing Insomnia — www.reversinginsomnia.com
6. Reversing Insomnia in 3 Days — www.reversinginsomnia.com
7. Drinking Water Guide — www.drinkingwaterguide.com
8. Drinking Water Guide-II — www.drinkingwaterguide.com
9. The Origin of the Earth's Water — www.drinkingwaterguide.com
10. Autobiography Of Dr. Rao M Konduru — www.mydiabetescontrol.com/Bio/

- Prime Publishing Co.

PLEASE WRITE A REVIEW ABOUT THIS BOOK

Now that you have read this book, please write a review about this book, and post your review on Amazon.

a. Please log into your Amazon account,
b. Search for this book "Reversing Insomnia in 3 Days, Author: Rao Konduru, PhD", or by using ISBN # 9780973112092, and click on the book cover & scroll down,
c. Click on "Customer Reviews", click on "Write a customer review" button, and "Create Review" box pops up.
d. Kindly write your REVIEW in the Write-Your-Review box, type a Headline, and click on 5 stars overall rating (you can give up to 5 stars).
e. Click on "Submit" button, and your review will be registered on Amazon.
f. Amazon will acknowledge your review with an email confirmation!

Thanks for posting your review!
Your opinion counts!

YOUR OPINION COUNTS!

Kindle eBook Is Available on Amazon

You can read this book on your computer, laptop, tablet, e-reader, iPhone, or any Kindle device by purchasing Kindle eBook. It is available on Amazon.
Please log into your Amazon account, and search for "Reversing Insomnia, Kindle eBook" or by using ASIN #.

The end of the book "Reversing Insomnia in 3 Days".

BEST WISHES!

www.ingramcontent.com/pod-product-compliance
Lightning Source LLC
Chambersburg PA
CBHW080004280326
41935CB00013B/1747